MORE NOTARY EDUCATION RESOURCES FROM QUID PRO BOOKS

Books

Sold online in paperback & hardback, and at leading ebook sites:

Louisiana Notary Exam Sample Questions and Answers 2025: Explanations Keyed to the Official Study Guide, by Steven Alan Childress (2025)

Louisiana Notary Exam Outline 2025: A Simpler and Shorter Study Guide, by Michele Childress (2025)

Louisiana Notary and Legal Forms with Explanations, by Michele Childress and Steven Alan Childress (2024)

Become a Notary Public in Louisiana: Process and Possibilities, by Steven Alan Childress (2025)

Louisiana Civil Law Dictionary, by Gregory W. Rome and Stephan Kinsella (2011)

Webinars

Remote education found at *www.SchoolOfNotary.com*, and registered with the Secretary of State:

"School of Notary" full-length weekly class on Zoom and recorded

"The Big Picture" overview seminar

"The Final Lap" summation/review seminar and sample-exam workshop

"I Passed – Now What?" practical seminar for newer notaries

LOUISIANA NOTARY EXAM
SIDEPIECE TO THE 2025 STUDY GUIDE

Tips, Index, Forms —
Essentials Missing in the Official Book

Steven Alan Childress

QUID PRO BOOKS
New Orleans, Louisiana

Copyright © 2025 by Steven Alan Childress. All rights reserved. No part of this book including the annotated index and forms may be reproduced or shared, in any form including copying of the digital files, without written permission by the author.

Published in 2025 by Quid Pro Books.

ISBN 978-1-61027-518-7 (trade paperback)
ISBN 978-1-61027-515-6 (hardcover)
ISBN 978-1-61027-516-3 (mass mkt. pbk.)

QUID PRO BOOKS
5860 Citrus Blvd., Suite D
New Orleans, Louisiana 70123
www.quidprobooks.com

This information is provided to aid comprehension of notary practice and procedure, and of the Louisiana notary examination and its official study guide, and should not be construed as legal advice or the practice of law. Please consult an attorney for inquiries regarding legal matters. For information on how to contact the author about this guide (corrections are welcome), see the *About the Author* section at the end of the book.

Publisher's Cataloging-in-Publication

Childress, Steven Alan.

    Louisiana Notary Exam Sidepiece to the 2025 Study Guide: Tips, Index, Forms—Essentials Missing in the Official Book / Steven Alan Childress.

    p. cm.

    Includes annotations, forms, and index.

    Series: *Sherpa Series*

1. Notaries. 2. Notaries—United States. 3. Notaries—Louisiana. 4. Notaries—Louisiana—Handbooks, Manuals, etc. I. Title. II. Series.

KF8797 .C43 2025   2025895447

Cover design copyright © 2025 by Quid Pro, LLC. The "Sherpa Series" image of the munching mountain goat, Sherpa, is a trademark of Quid Pro, LLC, with original artwork copyright © by Mary Ruth Pruitt, used by permission and with the thanks of the author.

First trade paperback printing: February, 2025

Contents

1. Introduction: "Where's the Index?" 1
2. Why Become a Notary Public? 5
3. Crucial, Inviolate Rules Using the Official Study Guide 9
4. Registering and Taking the Exam; Important Exam Strategies 13
5. Study Strategies and More on Taking the Exam 23
6. Commonly Tested Concepts and Mistakes 27
7. The Four A's of Notarial Functions 47
8. Concept and Structure of the Authentic Act 53
9. "AA": Acts Required to Be Authentic Acts or in Authentic Form 57
10. Notarial Testaments and Successions 63
11. Acknowledged Acts 67
12. Index and Additional Definitions 71
13. Cross-referencing Expanded 89
14. Suggested Annotation Holes and Filling Them 93
15. Useful Lists to Insert into the Guide 97
16. Ambiguities in the Study Guide 101
17. Visualizing Community Property and Wills 105
18. Acts, Forms, and Exemplars 117
19. Notarial Practice Tips 129

About the Author 137

1
Introduction: "Where's the Index?"

The Louisiana notary examination is famously challenging. Still, everything you need to know to pass it is found somewhere in the state's official study guide.

Sort of. The content is all in there, true, but the organization and functionality of the guide—named *Fundamentals of Louisiana Notarial Law and Practice*—are notoriously nebulous. So the details are inside but often hard to find, harder to learn than necessary, and missing some essentials of any textbook—including a subject-matter index.

It's surprising that a book meant to be used in a time-pressured open-book exam omits the index. It's hard enough to learn the concepts and details without one, but especially difficult to find specifics during the exam itself. In a real sense the exam is a scavenger hunt for facts, some counterintuitive. Is the Louisiana civil code really the Napoleonic Code? (no) May a notary serve as executor of a will she wrote and notarized? (yes) May an absent heir appear through an agent's power of attorney to sign a small succession affidavit? (no) Can a settlor to a trust name herself as trustee? (yes) Is a notary disqualified for a DUI arrest? (no) Try finding that trivia fast in a 737-page book with no index.

The exam's much more than a scavenger hunt, of course. But it's *at least* that. An index would help a lot, both to take the exam and before that to learn key concepts. It's especially surprising that the index goes missing in the one book you're allowed to crack open the day of a four- or five-hour exam averaging a pass rate under 20%.

Couple that glaring omission with the relative lack of forms that notaries actually use in practice—examples of authentic acts, affidavits, powers of attorney, and the like—and you get the feeling that the examiners want you to construct *on the fly* the structure of a valid legal document. They don't, but they don't make it easy either.

I'm not really dissing the study guide. It's carefully written by leading authorities to be informationally complete, to be used fairly and uniformly the day of the exam, open-book. The content is impressive and interesting. The explanations are clear. It's such a profound resource that you'll find it on the shelves of every responsible law and notary practice, often in multiple years shown by a rainbow of covers. Last year's was black—you need the 2025 *gray* one. The answers to the 50-to-55 questions you'll face on the exam are found in *Fundamentals*; the examiners don't make you, technically, depend on any outside resource. But the fact remains that almost all test-takers need help. The exam's just that hard.

Why did they leave out the index? Several years ago the book *had* one, if incomplete; but they *removed* it! Even further back in time—when it was named the "Study Guide"—it was full of sample forms and acts, helping readers visualize the documents they were learning to draft. My guess is that the move toward an all-open-book test (initially it was closed-book, then one part was open, now yours is open fully) and an all-multiple-choice one (originally you'd write out acts and mortgages freehand) necessitated making the resource less useful the day of the exam. Or at least *perceived* to be one that could be taken just by going in with a book and its index (BTW, a fullproof fail tactic). I think they believe the exam is fairer for all if the book doesn't give away too many answers by telling you where in the book to find the exact rule they're testing. I also suspect they feel any index is unfair if it isn't 100% complete, because some answers could be tracked down from it while some could not.

A more cynical answer is to observe that the default position for a notary in Louisiana is to be an attorney first—in fact in many civil law countries (and Puerto Rico), *only* lawyers may be notaries. Our state may be generous in creating nonlawyer-notaries and vesting them with many powers that in any other state would be the illegal practice of law, like drafting wills and donations. But in essence nonlawyer-notaries are treated as the exception, not the rule, so it feels as if the exam is hard so that notaries without law licenses do not dominate the profession.

That may be an understandable policy for some non-cynical reasons, but the result seems to be the relatively consistent 15 to 23% pass rate (for most exams after 2011) even as the number of exams per year increased and the format became open-book with no written component. Be thankful it's not December 2010, when 14 of 602 takers statewide became notaries (2%—gulp), or even March 2021 (6%). While practically all lawyers who want to become one easily do, for just a small fee.

Anyway, the text now *feels* a little like what hardware designers call *crippleware:* a product like a computer chip or car that is kept sluggish by a simple switch, while the costlier souped-up model merely activates the switch. The big gray book's not, to be fair, "crippled" in its present form. But it's missing some relatively simple switches to make it much more functional.

There's no substitute for studying hard and reading *Fundamentals* close enough that your mind becomes at least a general index. This book doesn't claim to be a shortcut to passing. But exam-day will be less head-spinning, at least, with key components like a detailed index added to the official guide. The process of annotating the book is educational in its own way. And studying along the way will make more sense, and be more efficient, with help beyond the study guide.

This book doesn't necessarily replace an organized course of study such as a prep class. It's not a workbook (Fred Davis's are famous and useful) or an interactive resource like classwork. Some such courses are online (such as one offered on Zoom by my wife Michele and me). Some are classroom-driven: most of these are offered privately while a few are part of a college-credit program (like Fred's at ULL and mine at Tulane).* A complete listing of registered notary educators, both remote and in-classroom, is found at the Secretary of State database: www.sos.la.gov/NotaryAndCertifications/NotaryEducationProviderInformation/Pages/default.aspx. Facebook groups—easy to find and join—offer dialog, advice, and opportunities to form study groups. This book also isn't a comprehensive explanation of the state textbook: you'll find that with Michele's *Louisiana Notary Exam Outline 2025: A Simpler and Shorter Study Guide*.

Students may learn best by formal study, concepts explained orally, or intensive self-study in extra resources—better than reading the state text on their own. Taking practice exams is very helpful, too, so classes or workbooks that provide those are ideal.† This book is meant to be a companion to the state text for self-study—or, we hope, an additional reading to be assigned or recommended in classes. That's why we made it affordable compared to them.

Taking classes doesn't guarantee passing the notary exam, of course. Still, this doesn't make them a waste at all—students without the instruction likely fail at a higher rate. But it does caution that organized coursework is—I'm full circle here—no substitute for studying hard and reading the study guide more than once. The website to Loyola's prep course (by experienced teacher Wendall Hilker) says it well: even for a 16-session course held February to June, "Please note that successful preparation for the exam will require extensive reading outside of the classroom."

One program is not enough. The official textbook is not enough. This book may not be either … but we hope it helps pull the other resources together and makes exam prep more sensible and organized. We especially hope that those who can't schedule or afford a prep course use this book to give the exam their best shot. At the very least, the *one weird tip to a fatter wallet* shared at the end of ch. 4 about filing fees could save you over a hundred dollars, paying for our books.

In addition to providing the essential missing material to be inserted into the official book and used on exam day, this companion guide also shares tips for prep and for test-taking, commonly tested subjects, typical mistakes, and conceptualizing the all-important authentic act and other forms—all keyed to the

---

* Besides such full-length classes, Michele and I offer shorter, affordable seminars to introduce concepts and the exam ("Big Picture") or review the subject and workshop a practice exam ("Final Lap"), at *www.notarysidepiece.com*. These are given remotely by Zoom or recorded. For a well-regarded in-person review/workshop held in Lafayette on a Saturday a few weeks before the notary exam, consider Fred Davis's Pass My Notary seminar. People learn in different ways, and there are many good options out there to study beyond the state textbook. In *Become a Notary Public in Louisiana*, ch. 11, I discuss in detail the workbooks, flashcards, classes, several notable teachers, and other resources available to prepare for the exam.

† After the first *Sidepiece* edition was released in early 2020, I published a companion volume. It is entitled *Louisiana Notary Exam Sample Questions and Answers: Explanations Keyed to the Official Study Guide*. Rather than just having an answer key to the questions, it details the right *and wrong* answers for each question, including the logic or "trick" examiners often use; test-taking tips are illustrated by examples. Its previous editions are updated for 2025. Our online class also offers four practice exams—different from those in my book—with feedback.

2025 study guide. The much-tested notarial testament and community property are explained and illustrated. The goal is to make sense of an exam that, more and more, asks you to approach a question by finding an answer that touches on several different parts of the permitted book (as detailed in ch. 4 below).

For what it's worth, I'm in a relatively unique position to comment on the process of becoming a Louisiana notary. I've taught law for years and once practiced it—yet, like many law profs in our state, hold my law license elsewhere. But when I wanted to become a notary and offer such services in my university and outside, the Secretary of State didn't care that I'm a California attorney (nor should they): courtesy appointments are for Louisiana lawyers only. I'd have to take that daunting exam. Sure, I had a headstart in law, but still needed to read that book carefully to get the notary details they test. I found it essential to index the book. I needed to make sense out of community property and wills. I found it helped to anticipate the "scenarios" they examine. I took lots of practice exams.

It's admittedly odd for an attorney to prepare for and take this exam. As far as I know, the other teachers of notary exam prep are either Louisiana lawyers, so they never took the exam. Or nonlawyers who took it when the exam was in a completely different format and the official text was differently organized—and they keep teaching it for the way *they* prepared and got tested. I hope my sweating through the *actual* format and content that's tested nowadays, using the *current* form of the study guide, makes this a fresh and instructive sidepiece to the official book. You decide.

This book is also meant for new and existing notaries—including attorneys—who may find useful its practice advice (ch. 19) and "big picture" on the four notarial A's and the structure of wills (ch. 7-11), as well as visualizing the will's relation to community property (ch. 17). Most of all, many practicing notaries buy the new *Fundamentals* edition each year, and consult it for the many acts and areas of law that come before them. They may want an expanded list of acts required to be in authentic form (p. 60 below). They could use expanded cross-references. At the least they need an index to the study guide, especially since the vital information on a topic is often found split across two or more parts of it.

2

Why Become a Notary Public?

To pass the exam, you have to be truly committed to the process. It helps to know in your core why you want to become a notary. The answer shouldn't just be that a boss suggested a raise if you get that commission, or a non-Louisiana company thinks being a notary is no big deal and is asking you to do it (a point suggested to me by former Jeff Parish examiner Karen Hallstrom). Or that it sounds like fun. I think it *is* fun, but that's not enough incentive to study extended hours beyond what is required in a prep course or seems normal for a professional exam.

But I did want to mention that there are many good reasons to become a notary, beyond the obvious job advancement or expanded responsibilities in an existing career. In career terms, another reason is public relations and client (or customer) development for yourself, apart from its positive impact on your specific job status. Having the seal draws people to you, at home or in the office. And those people perceive you, rightly, as a trusted professional for whom they can see future work in other spheres and give referrals to others. Most businesses kill for foot traffic; being known as a notary is a magnet for those feet.

There are also several new job openings and lateral moves available for those who are commissioned statewide as a notary, as you'll be. You can find work in real estate, law offices, government positions, automobile transfers and registration, and financial services that were not open to you before. One can strike out on one's own as a notary, not necessarily affiliated with for instance a real estate firm or a public agency, by opening a notary office or a mobile service yourself. Especially coupled with other self-employment or services, as with a mailbox-shipping store or as a consultant to hospice care and assisted living places, this can be part of making an independent, professional living. (Luckily, it's also a way to earn fees without their being subject to self-employment tax, and isn't a "profession" in the sense of paying a license tax, see guide p. 46; yet there's no doubt that the work is "professional" in every important way.)

There seems to be clear room in the market for mobile notary services fronted by an effective website using SEO and clear pricing quickly available to interested customers. Upfront pricing or fast quotes would draw clients. Perhaps the travel rate-setting on the website could be framed in terms of typical ride-sharing costs, in a way that clients would understand and feel comfortable paying beyond the cost of the notary or drafting service itself. At the least, getting on the lists of various mortgage providers who call you to do closings and refi packages makes a worthwhile side gig.

More importantly, there are many non-career reasons to set this goal. Pride of accomplishment is real and valid, and a profession is understandably respected; it's not just a job. People have heard how tough the exam is (well, not friends from other states, where notaries are just functionaries). The work itself requires care, precision, and trust. Drafting testaments and powers of attorney for those who need them protects families and finances for many who might not have such an instrument just when they could use it most. You'll do a lot of good. And as with other professions, you can cause a lot of damage if you don't know what you're doing or you act unethically or unprofessionally. See the movie *Body Heat* for the harm one can cause by mis-drafting a will (and because it's a great film), in that case for violating a Florida rule similar to Louisiana's prohibition against substitutions in a testament.

Notaries in *common law* states (and common law countries like England) do require trust in one important way: that the person who's signing is properly identified. That function is performed by Louisiana civil law notaries, too, but they do so much more (see pp. 54-55 in your study guide). The origin of the common law notary, beyond the church-witness function stated on p. 19, owes in part also to the need for the king to be sure the people who came before him were verified as who they claimed to be (say, not an assassin). It was a vital function, to be sure, but the identification-specialty this produced, quite unrelated to the practice of lawyers then, made the notary in effect the King's Bouncer.

You'll be far more than that. The *civil law* notary grew out of a wider need in society for the verification, creation, and preservation of vital documents related to property ownership and transfers, family matters, and courtroom evidence (see ch. 1 and 3 in the guide). The civil law notary was always connected to law, legal documentation, and courtroom proof in ways that make the notary public historically linked to the profession of lawyer. When you read the first seven chapters of the guide—about the history and functions of the civil law notary and of Louisiana's legal system—the main goal is to learn the terms, rules, and concepts for the exam. But read them with interest for what they say about the proud tradition you'll be joining and your vital place in the legal system.

Also, this is a position that you'll hold for life—all other states limit the term—at least if you report annually to the Secretary of State, stay registered to vote, and don't commit a felony. Plus it's one you can obtain later in life that will retain its value in your senior years. Most people don't go to med school or become CPAs at an age where it still makes sense to become a notary and the barriers to entry are manageable. You won't need three years of law school or heavy student debt.

Finally, as challenging as the exam is, there's no real limit on how many times you can take it. You don't want it to be like the bar exam for *My Cousin Vinny* ("Nope, for me, six times was the charm."). But it *can* be. The point is that it's a hard enough exam that there's no shame in failing it, or retaking it. You can go into it with the mindset that the pressure, though real, is mainly internal and not life-altering if more than one time is a charm. No one should *plan* on taking it over—especially if such thoughts tempt you to "wing it" or not do your honest best. But you could note parallels to the CPA process, by which all candidates know they must pass four separate exams. Even if the notary exam isn't truly four separate parts, passing after two or three administrations is more efficient and doable than what CPAs endure, if they even pass all four the first time.

Take some comfort in the fact that, as uphill as this exam feels, the effort is what *should* be expected of a "public officer" (p. 46) having such responsibilities and impact on people. Thinking "it's unfair this exam's so hard" only makes it harder to take it seriously enough to study each day, take extensive notes in your official book, learn from practice exams, use this companion guide to annotate your book in detail in preparation for the exam, and endure the four-hour exam itself.

At the end of it all, it'll be worth it.

3

Crucial, Inviolate Rules Using the Official Study Guide

The Secretary of State's website spells out the current rules for the day of the exam, including the prohibition on bringing food and drink into the test administration and the lack of a break in the five hours. They do let you use the bathroom, which may have a water fountain, but trips don't extend your time. (Lately they allow a new, clear bottle of water—no mugs, tumblers, coffee, or Cokes.)

The website also lists the process to apply in advance for deviations from the fixed rules as accommodations under the Americans with Disabilities Act. Consider those rules well before going to the exam. They won't give exceptions on the fly. More on game-day issues later, in the next two chapters.

More urgent to know right now are all the rules that apply to the *Fundamentals* book itself. They affect, right from the start, how you study and take notes.

Currently the exam is totally open book, in the sense that you can use the official study guide during the exam. **But,** during the exam:

- It can only be the *2025 edition* study guide for future exams administered in 2025. You won't be able to talk the examiners at the door into letting you use an older book, for *any* reason. Everyone has the exact same gray book on test day. And you can't use this *Sidepiece* book, or any other resource; that's why we advise indexing the state study guide itself and writing cross-references and notes *into* it.

- You can't *insert* pages or post-its, or otherwise supplement the book with loose sheets or attached material other than the original pages bound in the book. There's no pasting pages or "shipping type printed labels" into it. Proctors at check-in actually flip through each candidate's book and hold it by the spine to see if anything falls out. Even if the Secretary of State's office posts updates or errata to its website (they occasionally do), you should write them into the book rather than inserting a loose page.

- *Tabs* are allowed, but in a limited way spelled out on the Secretary of State's site. For example, the tabs must be the permanently-applied kind. Those are sometimes hard to find at office stores, which tout the repositional kind you *can't* use; I had to buy them online. They must be "clear" and a maximum of two inches. You can only use *one* tab on a page. "Clear" *does* allow see-through but colored plastic tabs (as pictured in a link from the website). Unless tabbing is important to your way of studying, there's no advantage to it over the indexing and cross-referencing suggested in this guide—in part because answers are often split across several spots in the book, not found just at one tab. At least, only use Post-Its at first where you *think* you'll tab, then later affix the permanent kind at spots you keep. Even if you do keep some of these temporary markers and put tabs there, consider putting the tabs at the top of pages so that you can still flip through the book easily during the time-pressured exam.

- No *electronic device* or phone can be on—and if they suddenly buzz or sound, as in rebooting on their own (or making a weather or Amber alert), you get kicked out, no refund! Keep in mind that friends may have apps that make your phone sound even when "off." Just leave it in the car. No smart watch may be worn, even set to off. Lately, their instructions even tell you that no watch of any kind is allowed.

Still, that leaves a lot you **can** do with your study guide, to make it even more "open" a book:

- You can write in the book as much as you want to, in ink or pencil, in whatever colors you wish. The words and annotations so inserted are not limited to your own original thoughts.

- You can write on the blank inside-cover pages and other pages that have blank canvases, in whole or in part. The cover insides are especially good spots to add vital information to have handy (see below at p. 93). And the current edition has lots of blank pages in back for notes—16 sides.

- You can use white-out over the print already in the book, to replace it with text that's more important, organized, or usable to you during the test. This process was crucial in previous years before they added blank pages. Ch. 14 below has some specific suggestions on where to white-out, if you do, and what to write. In that chapter, I argue there's still a place for creating space using the white-out method (and where) even while you use the new blank pages for other things. In ch. 12, I say why you shouldn't use up the blank pages for an index; it's better to insert it into their own glossary.

- You can highlight or color-code, including using color markers along the edge to create a tabbing effect without physical plastic tabs. Of course, don't over-highlight. "Bible highlighters" don't bleed through the page.

In the process, turn the guide into what you want it to be, within the limits of these rules. It'll be more functional than in its original form. It makes little sense to take a lot of notes in a notebook or on a laptop, unless that's just a waypoint to adding the right ones—the best ones—somewhere into the guide itself. *You can't take the notebook in with you*, or print-outs from your typed notes. So I don't recommend you waste energy creating notes that can't be accessed—since you are perfectly permitted to take notes in the book itself up to its physical limits.

While making notes in the book, I suggest using a fine-point mechanical pencil with hard lead and a good eraser. You'll probably have some false starts and misprints along the way that are best changed easily. Ink is all right (but not erasable ink—it disappears under heat!), but be prepared to resort to white-out when you realize you have better points to make than the ones you started with. Such tips are detailed in ch. 5 below.

You could go overboard with the notion that the study guide is a canvas. But to some extent it really is that, and you can make it work for you.

A Few More Tips on Using the Official Study Guide: Law English

Some legal terms or other wordings used in the *Fundamentals* book tend to confuse students. A little de-coding may be helpful. I don't mean substantive law terms like those that are discussed in the textbook or defined in the glossary in back of it. I mean other words that people in law use all the time that are tossed into *Fundamentals* as if the whole world already knows them. When you see these in the book, or in notary practice, here's the code:

- *supra* means *above*—and *infra* means *below*, like later in a case opinion.
- *Id.* is a signal that repeats a citation (from a case or statute) that was just cited. Just look to the last citation (often a line or two up from the *Id.*) and read this as "the same citation you just said." In English lit, it's *Ibid*.
- *ff.* means *following*, like the next pages. So, referring you to pages 38ff. means you should look at 38 and also the following pages. The same thing is done with statutes by saying *et seq.* at the end of the number, meaning "and so on."
- A *foreign judgment* may refer to an out-of-state one, depending on the context—not necessarily a non-U.S. one. Yes, in this sense California is foreign. *Judgment* in this context means a final, formal decision of a court. Courts may justify their decisions with an *opinion*, often just called a *case*. That's right: the word *case* could mean the entire dispute between parties *or*, confusingly, the written result of it. "I am reading an important case that resolved the whole case. So get off my case already."
- Judges along the way may also issue *Orders*. In Louisiana, these tend to be called *Rules*, as on p. 321. As in "Judge Diaz issued a Rule to Show Cause today." As a notary, you won't draft proposed Rules for the judge to sign, but you'll often notarize a party's affidavit that supports a proposed Rule. This is different from the "rule" or "holding" that a case sets.
- *Conventional* tends to mean contractual, by agreement, by convention of the parties (like how treaties are called Conventions). In context, it probably doesn't mean "ordinary" or "typical" as it often means in English.
- *Juridical* doesn't mean *judicial*. A judicial act is one done by a court. A juridical act is often done by a notary—not in court—such as a donation.
- *Legal* often means "by operation of law" rather than the opposite of "illegal." E.g., a legal mortgage (p. 289) doesn't mean one that isn't forbidden. It's one that arises by law, rather than judicially or conventionally.

- *Special* usually means *specific*, not *super-amazing*. Special interrogatories are a set of questions given to the jury to answer ("Was driver exceeding the speed limit?"), more specific than just "liable" or "not liable." Special damages means specific ones, as opposed to general damages.

- *Interrogatories*, other than in the jury context just noted, are questions given to a party during the pre-trial litigation phase called *discovery*, usually in civil cases, not criminal ones. The party then answers the questions under oath (the verification noted at p. 633), which is useful for investigation of the facts and to cross-examine the witness at trial (to "impeach" them if their answers deviate from the pre-trial ones).

- *Civil* in one sense refers to the civil law, here meaning Louisiana law, as opposed to the common law derived from England. But the term *civil* when meant to refer to cases or litigation—"the wrongful death case is in civil court"—means that it's not a criminal case. A *civil action* is a private dispute between parties (sometimes including the government as a party) rather than a charge *by* the government *against* a person for a crime.

- *Authentic* doesn't mean "real," really. It refers to the evidence-law process of *authentication* (identification and verification of its genuineness) that documents have to go through in court to have them "admitted into evidence" and be considered as proof. But in Louisiana *authentic acts* (as well as *acknowledged acts*, both introduced below in ch. 7) don't need an in-court witness to authenticate them. They can be considered as proof without any witness vouching for them; so, they are "self-proving." That doesn't mean the judge or jury has to believe them. But at least the documents are there for their consideration, efficiently produced in court. This creates a role for the Louisiana notary—drafting and verifying documents out of court that can be used in court without more—that doesn't exist in other states. The authentic act (ch. 19) is a civil law wonder.

- *Mandate* may mean a power of attorney (ch. 15); or, by a court or other legal actor, it can be an Order. "This mandate will issue immediately."

- *Parol evidence*, mentioned on p. 321, means oral evidence, as opposed to written documentation or proof. There's a real issue in contracts law as to whether parol evidence may be used to deviate from the clear terms of a written contract (p. 161). But of course there are many situations when it's OK to have an oral contract with no writing whatsoever.

In addition, there are numerous legal terms in the civil law or Louisiana law, discussed in the study guide, that have a meaning different from how the word sounds in common parlance. Examples: *naked* owners, *real* rights, and *vulgar* substitutions. We collect and explain those below at p. 46. Like the above, these are key to know for understanding what you're reading in the study guide. Plus the terms we lay out in ch. 6 below, and some above like *conventional* and *legal*, are highly testable precisely because they are counterintuitive.

4

Registering and Taking the Exam; Important Exam Strategies

Registration and Pre-Assessment

The process of becoming a Louisiana civil law notary is laid out for you on the Secretary of State website, along with all the specific annotation rules for the study guide just discussed.* The process picks up from the formal prerequisites of a notary found on p. 64 of the official book, which must be learned not only to apply in the first place but also because they're testable requirements for all notaries. (See also the statutory appendix, App. A, at pp. 669-70.)

These qualifications include being 18-plus with a high school diploma or equivalent; in-state residence; registered to vote (for citizens); no felony record unless pardoned; and proficiency in English. Assuming you meet these minimums, which you verify in an account opened on the website ("Application to Qualify"), you register and take the Notary Exam Pre-Assessment online (only once). This short reading comprehension exam has zero to do with notaries or law. It's merely informational and advisory—but it's a good heads-up on reading weaknesses you may have that you realistically need to improve to pass the real notary exam.

When? It takes about a week to get that feedback, then you can register for the exam itself (*a month* or more before its administration). By law, the exam must be given at least twice a year, though sometimes it's been offered as many as four times. For 2025, an exam is scheduled to be given May 17 (after one already held January 11—an atypical timing)—if feasible for all entrants to be accommodated. If not, they'll do a spillover administration June 7, as they often need to do (and probably will because of the long gap between January and May). When you register for the May 17 exam, you need to keep June 7 open, because you won't know till about ten days before May 17 whether you get assigned to that date or the other. They don't accept requests for one date or the other, for any reason (even Covid). They don't refund your $100 registration fee if you can't make the assigned date. This may require you to make hotel reservations for two Fridays.

This administration (either May 17 or June 7) will use the traditional process of everyone taking the exam together on one date, with a paper exam, answering on

---

* "Laid out," but most people say it's confusing. So I wrote a preliminary book on registration tips, the multiple steps, exam structure, and info anyone would want to know before committing to the profession and process. It's called *Become a Notary Public in Louisiana* and has a 2025 edition explaining the newer on-computer plan in detail.

scantrons using #2 pencils you bring to the site. The sites are Baton Rouge and Alexandria only (in the past they used Shreveport, too, but not this year). You are emailed about ten days in advance not only the specific date but also the location and exact check-in time for you. They are staggered and specific enough to you that if you show up late, they won't let you in, even if others are checking in at that time.

For the May exam, it doesn't matter how early you register as to which date you get (main date vs. spillover). You can't really "game" their assigned date, as the assignment seems random and not at all dependent on date of registration (though usually more people are assigned to the earlier date, as the later one is truly used for overflow, so odds are that you'll take it May 17). Also, keep in mind that the two exams are completely different; later test-takers get no real advantage from reading about what was tested the a few weeks earlier.

They have not named, yet, any later test dates in 2025—but they will. The stated plan (announced in a notary educators' meeting last year), if they can implement it in time, is for subsequent exams to be administered on computer without a paper copy, and no scantrons. At first the location will only be LSU in Baton Rouge Himes Hall), with hopes to expand to LSU-A fairly soon after. The timing will be by reservation at specific times made available in the week, and some Saturdays, rather than everyone at one public test date. Each exam will be randomly generated, so that people in the same test room have different tests, and other people on different days do too. Each exam is drawn from a pool of some 900 questions they have used in the past and know how hard they are, so the algorithm can create each exam having about the same difficulty overall as the next. No pencils will be needed, but you'll still be able to use the study guide. Presumably they will provide scratch paper, since there's no test booklet and you're not allowed to write into the study guide during the exam.

Keep an eye on the SOS website for any new dates (or the new system of rolling dates) and even for changes to these posted dates. Check it regularly, or watch Facebook groups. The SOS website is unlikely to hint at a further date in 2025, past June, until May or so once they decide whether to use the new process or instead have another traditional scantron administration first. My best guess is that the new process will be in place by July and announced in May, but hopefully the SOS will tell us sooner on their website. The prediction is that the new system will run through mid-November (then March-November in 2026) and allow people to sign up for multiple exams if spots are available (perhaps limited to one try per month). This is a lot more shots at it than the traditional system allowed. Probably the random exam will have 50-55 questions in four hours (as opposed to most previous exams of 70-80 questions in five hours. We'll know for sure once they start implementing it and announce details on the website.

Where? The May/June administration uses two locations: Baton Rouge and Alexandria. New Orleans as yet offers no test site and probably will not, and it may be a while before they return to Shreveport. For all exams, the site they choose for you is based on proximity to your home address, but there's a lot of leeway. If you live close to one of the sites they use, you'll get that one (e.g., New Orleans people always get Baton Rouge), but if you live somewhere between two (e.g., just south of Natchitoches), there's no predicting which of the two they'll give you. Some report being assigned to one location for one exam but a different one on retaking it, without having moved. Presumably Shreveport and Ruston candidates will be assigned to Alexandria. Often Lafayette and Lake Charles candidates get Alexandria, but it may be that in the future they will shift those toward Baton Rouge since now LSU-A has to accommodate northern Louisiana people which previously had LSU-S. We'll know more when the new plan starts.

Just as with the precise date you're assigned between the main exam and a spillover one, your test *location* between the two cities is not told to you until fairly last minute. You may be emailed the chosen test site a week or two before the exam: they say "where to report" like you've been drafted into the Army. So there's little time to plan if you're not close to one site. You may want to email LSU's Office of Testing & Evaluation, otes@lsu.edu, to request a change if you have a compelling reason (e.g., you go to school near a different site). They are more likely to accommodate a location change than a change of date.

This means you may need to make cancellable hotel reservations in two locations, if you happen to be somewhere that could be assigned to either—and of course two dates, because you may be assigned to overflow. So, four hotel dates.

All of this will be updated on the state website, so check that regularly. *Early registration is advised, and certainly waiting till the last day (say, April 17 for the May exam) can easily be too late—risking a computer glitch or the system thinking you have not already taken the preassessment.* Oh, and several of these online steps cost you money. Of course.

Exam Format and Test-taking Tips

The traditional format has been 70 to 80 questions, all multiple choice. But the January 2025 exam had 55 questions, still allowing five hours. The current website says it will be five hours but does not say how many questions. Most likely the May/June exam will have about 55 questions in five hours, but don't be shocked if they revert to the previous method of about 72 one last time. In the future, using the computer-based exam, there will likely be 50-55 in four hours.

For each question—almost always and as will continue with the computer-based exam—there are *four* options to choose from (with a smattering of questions offering five choices). It is never just two or just true-false. It's true that some questions will be worded in terms of true-false options, but still leaving four or five choices for you to pick from. For example, after a statement of facts or reference to a scenario, the call of the question may be something like: "Which one of the following [four or five] statements is false?" Or "All of the following require an authentic act, except: ..."

One format they've used makes choice D or E as "None of the above" or "All of the above." Yet the set-up to all questions (in bold face at the top of the exam) is to choose the "best answer." In exam-creation, it is not considered best practice to combine the general "best answer" instruction with a specific question that includes "None of the above," because there may be some reason that one of the other choices is not perfect but the others are very wrong—so, is "none" the best choice, or is it the imperfect but better option among the other two?

Or the general instruction confuses you with "D. All of the above," because you may believe that one of the options in A through C is clearly better than the other two. So the best answer might be, say, C. But none is actually wrong. Do you choose C as "best" or is "all" in fact best?

My best advice is that if the first three options are all wrong, even for some technical or picky reason, choose "D. None of the above," even though some are way more wrong than others. But if there's a fair case to be made that one answer is barely correct, if imperfectly stated, choose it rather than "none." And for "All of the above," use it even if one answer is not great. The good news is that they're likely to offer "all" in a situation where you can already tell that *two* of the options are correct. If you're right about that, it doesn't matter that you can think of a way to read the third choice as wrong; pick "D: All of the above."

Fortunately they don't use the "all" or "none" options too often in one administration (and it's unlikely to come up a lot in a randomly created computer-based exam in the future). Hopefully if they do, it will be pretty clear what they want you to pick as the right answer, assuming you know the information tested or can find it in the *Fundamentals* study guide.

As suggested above, some questions are worded in a globally positive or negative way, such as: "Which of the following statements is false?" This format tests your ability to know (or find) choices from *several places in the book*, because the options don't have to be related in subject matter to each other. It may help to write "TRUE" at the end of each option you think is true, reducing the options to the likely false one. Under test pressure it's easy to quickly mark the first statement that you're confident is correct—forgetting that you're supposed to pick the *false* one. I made that mistake on several practice exams (as have my students) until I made myself write "true" and "false" next to each option A through D, then went back to the call of the question above that, to remind myself they want the false one. And similarly where the call of the question is "Which of these statements is true?": read, and write "T" or "F" next to, *all* the choices.

Even outside the true-false format with four options, many questions force you to use two or more different places in the book to answer the question as a whole. They can do this by breaking down the information *in the book* over two places; an example is the law of mortgages, split between ch 18 and 21 in the study guide. Or the question itself makes you relate together two different rules to merge into one answer. Example: this small succession is an affidavit; affidavits can't be done via power of attorney (p. 98 below); therefore, answer C is wrong because it's having an agent sign for one of the heirs on the succession form. Either way, study and mark up the book in such a way that you can quickly go to multiple pages, to read the right answer or to merge two ideas into one right answer. This is another reason to index your book, as we explain in ch. 12.

Most questions are based on fact patterns they give you of people doing things, called "scenarios." These short hypotheticals tell a story of a transaction, event, or goal someone is trying to accomplish. The SOS site makes it sound like *all* the questions are based on "scenarios" which in turn may rely on "libraries" of incomplete or incorrect forms (which they provide you above the question asking about it). To be sure, they've moved in the direction of scenarios more than in many years past (and away from library documents very recently). But the website's emphasis on the scenario format obscures the fact that 5 to 10 or so of the questions are likely to be unconnected to any scenario or library of paperwork. They are straightforward questions about your knowledge of notary practice, court structure and jurisdiction, Louisiana law in covered areas like property, acts not supplied in a library, property descriptions, the civil law system, and even Louisiana history and geography related to the civil law.

These are standalone questions (rather than, elsewhere in a paper-based exam, a series of questions based on one fact pattern—which won't happen with randomly generated exams after June). These are much like the legacy general-knowledge questions they used to test in a closed-book format. So you can't ignore the study guide's introductory ch. 1-7 just because it'd be hard to test these subjects via a scenario. Be happy these are in reality low-hanging fruit if you can recall the right answer (e.g., that the signature is your "seal," p. 74) or, easier still, just know enough to locate and confirm the right answer that's quoted for you in the guide. The exam would be harder if they meant it when they suggest every question derives from a complicated fact pattern.

They certainly are moving to a system where each question will be tied to a unique scenario for that question only, not using it over a series of related questions. To make that manageable in just four hours, they necessarily will have to use standalone questions, too, and some very short or simple scenarios.

Even when the questions *are* based on a scenario, it's often the case that a particular question is only *loosely* based on the scenario—that the latter is just a jumping-off point to get you to define a term or apply a rule in a way that could easily be asked without reference to the scenario. These feel like the scenario is more of an excuse to ask the question than a necessary part of it.

So it may add up that, along with the low-hanging ones noted above, fully ten of the actual questions you see (out of, say, 55 or 70) are pretty much standalone knowledge questions, or ones loosely related to a scenario, rather than analyze-the-complicated-scenario ones—despite the website's description. That doesn't mean they're easy questions, or all just trivia. But they can be approached in a straightforward way, especially using the indexing and referencing strategies shared further in this guidebook.

The scenario-based questions, too, make you use your ability to find relevant passages in the study guide and apply them to the inquiry at hand—here, in the form of a fact pattern or, occasionally, a sample part of a document (shown just above that question). *Recognizing* the issue raised by the fact pattern, and the type of form that is being referenced if they add one, is a crucial skill. The answer ultimately will be found somewhere in *Fundamentals*, but you won't know where to look—even after creating an index—if you don't "get" the question and identify the issue.

You have to see the big picture and understand concepts *cold* to be able to look in the right place—even to know what index term to look up. So this puts a premium on using the textbook and any prep course you take to *conceptualize* notary law and clauses in forms. For example, knowing what a personal servitude is, and that there are other types besides usufructs (though that's the main one tested), is more important than knowing their detailed differences, assuming you've noticed the differences in your guide and can locate the passages quickly despite test pressure. That reality changes the way you *study* for the test from how it used to be administered a few years ago.

When it was an exam of memorization, code-article identification, and form-writing, there were a lot of details to learn *by heart*. There's still a lot of that involved in the current administration. But you can study each page knowing that *specific* details they can test—for instance, that property records have to be filed in Orleans Parish within 48 hours, unlike the 15 days elsewhere (p. 59); or that there are only eight reasons you can disinherit a kid, p. 495—need only be learned enough to recognize an issue. (If Orleans is mentioned in the question about recordation, that means something; if a reason is given for disinheriting a kid, you know it's got to be on the statutory list.) Once you make an index to find the right spot, the tiny *detail* they're testing (say, this deed was filed too late for Orleans; or daughter in the military hasn't talked to testator in years, but that doesn't let him cut her out of the will) can be quickly found during the exam.

There's still a lot of memorization necessary. But it's about learning the framework and general terms well, which is simply a different approach from what worked in years past. Study time is better spent learning the *forest* and projected subjects they test—and turning the book into a ready reference—than in quizzing yourself on the eight reasons for disinherison, or the seven documents that require a social security number. Turning the book into the reference resource is time-consuming, and this book offers no promise of less work. The point is that the time marking up your book in an engaged way (more on that in ch. 12-13 below) is more productive than flashcards, memory drills, and note-taking outside the confines of the study guide. Yes, it takes time to annotate the guide with a list of the seven social-security-number situations (p. 97 below); but you know if one comes up on the exam, and you've trained yourself to *recognize* the situation, you'll *find* their answer in a minute.

Our next chapter has more specifics on how the questions' format affects your study style and need to annotate the book. More exam-taking tips, especially about time-management, are also offered in the next chapter. In addition, detailed test-taking and format-deciphering tips are illustrated in application, in our *Louisiana Notary Exam Sample Questions and Answers 2025*, offering explanations of all the right and wrong answers—and why one is "best."

Exam-Day Process and Pitfalls

The day of the exam can be a grueling process, and not just because it's four or five hours long with no scheduled break. The test may delay some even to begin, because the check-in process for so many candidates takes time. (Even so, don't count on their letting you show up late just because your exam hasn't started.) Typically, even the end of the exam takes a few formal steps that make you stick around when you'd rather be getting a stiff drink.

Because no food or drinks are, technically, allowed during the exam, except at a water fountain during any bathroom breaks you may take (though lately they've allowed a clear water bottle at your feet), you may have some difficulty taking medicines along the way. Be sure to disclose your need to do so to the proctors during sign-in, so it doesn't appear during the exam that you are eating and to be sure to have access to water to take the medicine. If you need to be able to eat a bite during a five-hour stretch, for example because of blood-sugar issues, be sure to apply well in advance for accommodations under the ADA—don't' assume a last-minute exception. But even without accommodations, you may be allowed to go to the hallway to eat something, though that eats into your time.

Also, since the actual administration of the exam including sign-in usually takes more than the time of the test itself, prepare to go without food for a while. Eat sufficiently, but not too much, before the exam—including possibly a protein bar or similar portable food just before the check-in period starts. At least at the LSU testing building (Himes Hall), drink and snack machines are nearby to use just before sign-in. LSU-A probably has machines, too. *Important*: the exam rooms are notoriously freezing, especially Himes. Bring a jacket, sweater, or sweatshirt!

During the test, they enforce one important rule not given much attention ahead of time: you're not permitted to write *in* the study guide. You'll have to use your exam booklet as scratch paper (though after it's computer-based, they should provide paper and collect it at the end). They'll dismiss test-takers who write back into the official manual, believe it or not. It's likely their way to feel comfortable about reusing scenarios and questions without fear someone is spending the exam copying them for future students. In any event, you've spent months writing in it, so it could be old habit to jot a note as you take the test (for example, to remind yourself to come back to a place in the book). Make sure you do that only in the question booklet or other loose paper they give you!

As noted in chapter 3 above, they have strict rules on what objects you may bring into the testing room. Above all, don't have a device that could suddenly make a sound (even an *off* cellphone can decide to reboot and tell the world it's back on, or you may think it's off but it buzzes in a way easily heard in the quiet room). They'll kick you out if you have an active device, even if you didn't mean to.

Leave it in the car, if possible. *Print out* all required paperwork, especially your entry letter (in multiple copies and stash one in the car in case you forget).

At sign-in, you'll need the printed entry ticket or letter (an email they send about ten days before the first exam date), plus a valid and current ID such as Louisiana driver's license. They do *not* accept LA Wallet, so leave the phone behind. Apply now for a current ID! If your name on the ID is not the same as the one on your admission letter (the one used in your SOS account), contact the SOS Notary Division to work out a change or correction before the test date.

Bring plenty of sharp #2 wooden pencils, at least for the May/June exam using scantron. Even if you used mechanical pencils while studying, it's best to have the woody type at the test center. That is because the SOS notary office consistently *says* that you may not use mechanical ones they day of the exam. It's not on the webpage and I doubt they enforce it, but they have told that to people (including me) who call and ask. I suspect it's a preference more than a rule as such, out of concern that it won't be a #2 lead. Still, there's no reason to risk the intervention of an officious proctor: just take some regular pencils in with you.

Once time is called, stop writing immediately and sit there until your packet of materials is checked and all loose papers are collected. Do not write anything—or fill in *any* pencil dots on the answer sheet—after time is called. It is lore that people have been excused from the exam and their answers not graded (after all that!) simply for filling in one dot too late. Once the exam is computer-based, expect the program to time-out on its own, and likely provide a running countdown of remaining time since you're not allowed to bring a timepiece. To avoid being at risk of dismissal while using scantrons, keep an eye on the time on the test center's clocks (not your own watch).

Whether the test is on paper or computer-based, spend the last five minutes making sure you've answered every question asked. There's no penalty for a wrong answer, so there's absolutely no reason not to guess on the last few questions—or even fill in dots without looking at the question if you must—to make sure all questions get answered. You won't get counted off.

Passing Score

About a month later, or sometimes as much as seven weeks, LSU will send your result in a curt email. They intend for the grading time to be reduced to a week once they institute on-screen test-taking. Officially the passing score is 75% of the questions they count (excluding some rejected or experimental questions they toss in, often to try out for future exams). However, they reserve the right to adjust what passes after evaluation of all results and consideration of "post-test statistical analysis."

This has meant in recent years that in fact a score of 70% correct and above is considered to be passing. You can't know until you get your score, and they're only promising that 75% passes. But consistently they do wind up accepting many exams just below that score. I anticipate that this trend will continue under the new system as well, and that you'll need only a 70% to pass. But of course you should be shooting for the 75 (say, 41 of 55 right) regardless. Post-test analysis should continue under the new system, meaning they may throw out some question(s) on your own exam or adjust your score if it turns out you were generated an unusually difficult exam. They obviously intend for the exam to be generally as difficult for everyone, using the history of particular questions.

Receiving Your Commission and Saving on Fees

Once you pass, the SOS website tells you the final formal steps you need to go through to be commissioned in your parish of residence. Once again the requirements, covered on study guide pp. 64-69, are not just steps to take but are statutory mandates to learn for the exam itself. Mainly you'll need to file with the Secretary of State an oath of office, proof of a bond "or equivalent," and sample signature (your "seal"). Plus pay the SOS again, naturally. Congratulations!

The sample signature you submit does *not* have to be one that legibly repeats your full name. It could look like Prince's icon, for what it's worth (but clients are reassured if it's at least somewhat identifiable, so don't get too cute). It should be one that you can repeat consistently and comes naturally to you, so that you don't wind up writing something else by habit when you sign. I used to tell my students to use the one they sign checks with, but they were like "checks? ... what am I, 40?" At any rate, practice enough times that it flows from your pen.

The most typical "equivalent" of the surety bond is an Errors & Omissions policy ("E&O," to everyone). While the bond protects the Governor and is the minimum required, E&O goes further in insuring *the notary* against, well, errors and omissions you may make. It'd be worth the slight difference anyway (typically $8 more per year), but it actually pays for itself in a way not explained in the study guide or, surprisingly, by the SOS online....

Here's our "one weird tip" to save you $100 in filing fees during this process. In most parishes—almost all of them, as far as I could ascertain—the Clerk of Court charges that large fee (plus $5 if using credit card) to review and approve your proof of bond, which is a parish-wide documentation. (This is in addition to filing your oath of office with the Clerk and all the registration and test fees you pay online to the Secretary of State.) You then have to upload to the SOS site this proof you got the surety bond approved by your parish, to get commissioned—along with another SOS filing fee. But the Secretary *waives* proof of local bond-approval if you instead upload the coverage/declarations page for an *E&O policy* from a reputable company. (Because E&O policies are issued state-wide, they don't need to be approved by a parish clerk.) The E&O declaration must clearly show a five-year term of coverage, including a stated end-date, to avoid the parish charge.

So, since to the SOS, E&O coverage is "as good as" a bond (it's actually better)—and E&O is not reviewed by a parish for a large fee—the savings to a new notary is $100 minus the $40-or-less added cost of E&O over five years. That pays for this book, with change! The savings continue every five years, too, because again you'll have to prove to the SOS you have some acceptable coverage. And the only acceptable way to prove that with just a bond is via approval, expensively, by the clerk. There's just no good reason to get just a bond. And on p. 134, we discuss why you probably should go ahead and get $25,000 in coverage, at least.

Either way, you still have to file with your parish a notarized oath of office—but that should not cost as much to file as a bond does, if at all (parishes vary in whether they charge a filing fee for the oath, so ask them to waive it as a favor). Here you can save a little by only paying a notary to execute one form, not two. You may think you need two originals (one for the SOS, one for the parish), but you have *a month* to file the oath in the parish. Because the forms to receive a commission are easily done by scanning and uploading to your SOS account, you retain the original to later file locally. (In Baton Rouge, you can also deliver the required forms in person to the Secretary of State's notary division, though you still have to file your oath with the clerk of court for your home parish.)

Assuming you pay for the notary or other official to administer and verify the oath, the uploading method means you only have to get one oath notarized. More money saved. Also, your prep class teacher may offer to notarize your oath for free (and members of the leading Facebook groups offer this courtesy). Plus the oath may be administered and endorsed by another recognized state officer, who may not charge you as a notary public could. Such officers include justices of the peace and clerks of court. The oath form by the SOS is downloaded from https://www.sos.la.gov/NotaryAndCertifications/PublishedDocuments/NotaryOathOfOffice.pdf. The parish line at top is where you're signing it. The parish line later is where you're commissioned. A sample signature form is also at the SOS website, though any written and dated statement of that suffices.

Another way to save on fees in getting your commission, as well as during all the paid steps along the way, is to use a bank ACH payment. Then they don't charge you the $5 "convenience fee" each time, as they do with a credit or debit card.

5

Study Strategies and More on Taking the Exam

Chapter 3 above set forth the examiners' rules about how you can alter the study guide and still use it the day of the exam. Because all notes you can use must be written into the book—and not put on loose paper or inserts—it makes sense that note-taking should be done as much as possible in the book itself. This won't work if you have too many notes, or ones that take too much space to explain. So there's a premium on *efficient* note-taking, reducing the key concepts and rules to bulletpoints, sample forms, and visual guides like grids and flowcharts.

The rules also allow you to highlight at will. But obviously a page full of highlights won't make any key concept stand out. You'll need to stay disciplined to keep from over-yellowing the page (or any color). Some marginal notes that actually explain something—such as the "*AA*" that I recommend in ch. 9 adding to any discussion of a form or act that must be in authentic form—will be more useful the day of the exam than highlights.

Annotating your study guide. Even more useful during the pressure of the exam will be indexing and extra cross-references that help you find the relevant point of the book that lets you answer the question. So, time spent writing inside the book may help you less than committing to turning the glossary into a detailed index—as well as adding cross-references in the text itself where a form or context is discussed twice or more in the book, as often happens. These multi-located rules are very testable for two mutual but competing reasons: (1) if they repeat it the same in the book, it's important, or (2) often the rule or key point is not wholly repeated in two places, but rather only in one place is some *part* of it located and then the other place has *other* facets of the same subject. This means that you could find a place in the book during the exam where the subject is found, but only at the other spot(s) is the answer found to *this* question.

This examiners' trick requires that you extensively cross-reference the book and that your index be complete—not just have one reference or tab to where the term or rule is "mainly" discussed. Further, your added cross-references need to be by specific page number as much as possible, not just the first page of a general topic. There won't be enough time during the exam to read through a whole section when you could've already identified the specific idea on a named page. My suggestions on expansive indexing, and on additional cross-referencing besides what the study guide already offers, are detailed in ch. 12 and 13.

In addition to notes in the book as it exists, and creating an index and other referencing, there's a golden opportunity (really, a white-out one) to create more room for charts and notes near the location where the subject is discussed. Prep courses have long advised creating new real estate inside the study guide by whiting-out over parts of the book that aren't useful on exam day. The proctors do allow you to use white-out judiciously so as not to alter it in any major way from the outside. They flip through it to determine whether you've inserted paper or attached notes, or used the types of tabs they forbid, as explained on their website. Mainly that's done by turning the book upside down, holding it at the spine. It's not cheating to paint some pages and write over the new space. The best way to do this is a few thin layers, with pausing and a little blowing perhaps, to allow drying between. Slathering won't work right. Be cautious of using white-out *tape* if that can be seen as an "insert."

However, this standard tip of prep courses is less crucial with the current *Fundamentals*, since it adds 16 pages in the back for notes. Now, the main reason to use the white-out method of old is to have more notes near the actual location that's most relevant, if there are pages nearby that can be painted out with no loss of content (the material underneath is redundant or not particularly useful). Or to reserve the blank pages for class note-taking (or indexing, if you don't use the glossary for that—an option discussed in ch. 12). Some such suggestions, and what you may want to fill in there or at the back of the book, are discussed in ch. 14 below. Plus our ch. 15 has several *lists* of commonly tested rules that you *definitely* should write somewhere into your study guide.

It's best to take notes throughout the book in pencil. That way you can erase notes you find you don't need and correct mistakes as you go. A fine-point mechanical pencil (0.5mm, or certainly no more than 0.7, such as those from BIC) works best. But for any new surfaces you create with liquid paper, if you do, pencil works poorly and you may want to use a fine-point ballpoint pen (0.7mm, such as Zebra or Pilot). Gel ink and other slick pens won't stick to this surface.

Beware that erasable ink will disappear if you leave your book in a hot car. Even if you can resurrect some of it by using the freezer for two hours, it's best not to use erasable ink at all. You risk losing your hard-earned notes or indexing.

However you write notes, the goal should be just enough information that you can *remember* broad concepts, organization, and key points from the notes, then *find* details and rules the day of the test as needed, as explained below. The student with the *most* notes won't necessarily be the winner (and especially with the 2025 edition's many blank pages, it will be tempting to go overboard writing into the book). Your judicious and efficient use of bulletpoints, charts, and lists will be handy during the exam.

Regardless of indexing and note-taking inside the book, there's no substitute for *reading* all the chapters intently and repeatedly. Some more than others, as you see from the "testable areas" discussed below (ch. 6). Some of the chapters seem to be in the book mostly to lay a foundation for other, more-relevant and testable, parts. For example, probably the main reason the study guide has such an extensive discussion of suretyships and bonds in ch. 16 is because they test your understanding of the requirement that *notaries* buy a surety bond (pp. 65-67 in ch. 7). And ch. 18 on mortgages is important to lay the foundation for its application to notary practice in ch. 21. Most of the actual questions are likely to be drawn from the part that most clearly relates to notary law. But it's still important to write cross-references to the more general discussion so that, on test day, you can easily find the related points made there if they do ask about them.

It may sound trite to say the best study tip is to study hard, but anyone who offers some magic solution otherwise isn't being honest with you. Fortunately, as the previous chapter introduced, studying hard is not about memorizing every rule or nuance—you're allowed to *find* those during the exam—but more about understanding the concepts, contexts, and organization of the study guide so cold that you know what you're looking for even if you don't have it committed to memory.

As an example, there's no need to know by heart all the instances in which Orleans Parish practice differs from the rest of the state. It's OK if you've conceptualized why that may be true, and made a handy list of relevant pages in your indexing under "Orleans." To answer any question that turns on the location is just a matter of pinpointing it from the index. The same could be said for all the rules about when acts or forms need to be *recorded* in the clerk's office, not just signed at the notary's office. So the index in our ch. 12 lists multiple, detailed entries on "recordation." They tend to ask several questions, most likely two to three, that turn on recordation rules.

If anything, you may need to remind yourself during the test, rather than relying on memory, to search for a *confirmation* in the study guide of a rule you *think* you know. They often trick you by making the answer turn on some rule that actually has an exception, which you'd see if you be sure to locate the relevant place and look. Or the actual rule is counterintuitive, the opposite of something you thought you've known all along, e.g., doesn't the Secretary of State appoint the notary? Is our civil code "Napoleonic"? (No and no.) At worst, a quick look confirms your memory was right and gives you confidence for the next question. You don't want to spend more than a couple minutes confirming the easier answers—save time for the rest of the exam—but having a thorough index handy lets you locate the low-hanging fruit fast. Double-check even the "obvious" ones.

Time management. You should similarly go into the exam with a plan for how long you spend on any one question. Commit to spending no more than four to six minutes even on the hardest question, mark your best guess, move on, and come back to that one if you have time. 240 minutes divided by 55 questions is 4.36 minutes—or 5.45 if they give you five hours. Some easier questions (e.g., the commonly tested one that "heir" is used for an "intestate" succession) take far less and buy time ... but you also may need time for a bathroom break or two and a trip to the water-fountain.

Of course you won't waste focus actually timing each question, but you certainly can get a feeling that you're lingering on a hard one. It's better to return to it later than not to finish the exam, missing the chance at several closing questions. Meanwhile, though, mark the answer of your best effort for those 4.36 minutes (you probably did at least eliminate some answers and increased your odds), even if you think you'll come back to that one later. Don't make a habit of leaving blanks along the way. You can change the answer if you're *sure* you did it wrong the first time around—basically, only if you see the correct answer in the book itself or you realize a clear reason your guess was wrong. Otherwise, leave your five-minute, first-impression answer alone.

Taking practice exams not only helps you learn notary law and exam format, it also helps you develop a rhythm and an instinct about when it's time to move on to the next question. (For example, my Sample Questions book has four exams and explained answers, and our Zoom class administers four different practice exams on-screen, as they will soon do—optional but highly recommended.) I'd add you probably should not skip too many individual questions as you go, and certainly not get mixed up as to which ones remain.

"Best" answer? On any one question, be sure to read all the answer choices and not fixate on the first one that looks right. The examiners emphasize that it's a search for the "best" answer, not one that is right in some technical or limited way. They consciously include a "distractor" that is OK as far as it goes, or partly right, but doesn't fully resolve the essential issue in the question—and doesn't count. It may be right for a narrow reason when the larger concern you can see they are trying to test by the question as a whole is not met. Or it is a statement true in the abstract but doesn't really apply to this scenario.

In reality, most questions (by far) have only one right answer, and this dilemma of the tempting distractor at worst narrows you down to two decent options. So it shouldn't intimidate you too much. Just be aware of how they do that at times and the need to read all choices. This feeds back to my suggestion, above at p. 16, of writing 'true' or 'false' next to statements in A through D, to keep it all straight as you go.

Margin of error. As challenging as one stretch of the exam may seem, or the exam as a whole even, keep in mind that there's a decent margin of error to earn a pass. Since 70% usually passes, and you'll probably face around 55 questions, you can miss 16 questions and still pass! Knowing this should ease the pressure some, especially for any one question that risks bogging you down (say, a tough property description one). I recognize that not all of the 55 questions are necessarily scored, as some are experimental (tried out for future use), but the logic of this *ratio* still applies: if all 55 counted, you'd need to get 39 right, and so on for smaller numbers. You can set a realistic goal for any one question, or any one stretch of questions, and not be overly intimidated.

6

Commonly Tested Concepts and Mistakes

Terminology and Definitions

Terminology is often tested, but usually not through such a straightforward way as repeating a definition from the glossary. It's useful to re-read the glossary and learn the definitions of legal phrases and other terms of art (and possibly use the short, handy, and affordable book *Louisiana Civil Law Dictionary* to nail them down). But legal terms are tested more indirectly—by their application in a scenario that won't make sense if you don't know the glossary well. The examiners especially like to use words in the midst of a scenario that are hard to keep straight if you haven't studied hard those terms that differentiate the parties to a transaction, terms that aren't necessarily intuitive.

The most obvious set of legal terms that are mutually confusing and involve people involved in legal matters are: actors' roles ending in *–or* versus *–ee*. It is crucial to know, for instance, what a scenario means by mortgag*or* versus mortgag*ee*. Offhand you may think that the one who provides a loan to someone buying the house is the mortgagor; after all, they're the one making the loan that is the underlying goal of the mortgage. But in fact the mortgagor is the one making the mortgage (the promise to repay), so that's the borrower and buyer. Another confusing set is less*or* versus less*ee*. Which one's the landlord?

Really, though, the terms make sense if you remember this one rule of thumb we've taught in law schools over the years: *–or* and *–er* mean the one who is *giving* the interest, property, or legal device. While *–ee* designates the one who *receives* it. You already know this hint when you use it in more common contexts you've used all your life. You already know employer and employee. Even if both benefit and give something to the transaction, the one who gives *employ*ment is the employer; the one who receives employment is the employee. Knowing the easy terms, you can analogize to less-known pairs like lessor-lessee. The one who gives the lease is the landlord, called the lessor; the tenant who receives it is the lessee. Don't think for a minute that a lessee can dictate the lease to the landlord.

Another pair that's easy to see is grantor versus grantee. A grantor gives (grants, for example an easement), while a grantee receives the grant. It's the same with payor-payee: the payee receives the money. Now just play the same trick on other paired terms that you don't already know or can't as easily figure out. So:

- Mortgagor gives a mortgage (and may be the only one who has to sign), while mortgagee takes it and is thus the lender. In the typical transaction, the mortgagor is the home-buyer. This pair is the hardest but most tested.

- Obligor gives an obligation (like owing child support) to an obligee (receiving payment)
- More examples are stated in abbreviated form below.

Also, you can remember the difference by noting that the giv*er* ends in the *–er* form (same as *–or*; ends in *r* like giv*er* does). While the word *receives* has two "long e" sounds in it, just like *–ee* (so, *receive* rhymes twice with *–ee*).

I hope this concept makes it easier to differentiate confusing pairs on the fly during the exam. But just in case, you could write, near the first glossary page or anywhere easily found on test day, several of these:

    grantor=one who gives / grantee=receives the grant
    donor=one who donates / donee = receives donation
    m'or =borrower=home-buyer / m'ee=lender=bank
    lessor=landlord / lessee=tenant
    vendor=seller / vendee=buyer
    creditor=gives credit to a debtor
    assigner=one who assigns / assignee=gets the transfer
    drawer=one who gives check / drawee=receives it=bank→then pays to payee

In addition to confusing pairs, there are other definitions that seem to be most testable, as listed below. If they're not in the glossary already, they should be inserted as part of your expanded index, as detailed below (ch. 12), and adding cross-references in the book to where they are defined or applied (ch. 13). Learn them! Such core terminologies include:

- Donation *inter vivos* vs. donation *mortis causa* (a testament or will)
- Donations that require authentic act vs. onerous donation vs. remunerative donation vs. "giving in payment" (*dation en paiement*)
- Cash sale vs. credit sale (act of sale with vendor's lien) vs. sale with mortgage
- Conventional mortgage vs. collateral mortgage
- Predial servitude vs. personal servitude
- Dominant estate vs. servient estate
- Usufruct vs. naked ownership
- Mandate vs. procuration
- Movables vs. immovables
- Authentic act vs. authenticated (acknowledged) act (ch. 11, below)
- Intestate vs. testate succession (ch. 10 and 17, below)

- Inheritance vs. legacy; heir vs. legatee [these roles are tested *a lot*]
- Succession by affidavit vs. judicial succession (the one they stress notaries may not do)
- Community property vs. separate property
- Provisional custody by mandate vs. non-legal custodian's affidavit vs. designation of tutorship
- Corporation vs. LLC vs. partnership
- Act of correction by parties vs. act of correction by notary
- Point of beginning vs. commencing point (for property descriptions)

These testable distinctions ought to be learned cold, with no need to find a definition in the book. Search the guide instead for finding detailed rules about it or applications of it.

Testing Recent Changes in Notary Law

Notary prep courses emphasize that topics are very testable when they've had a change in the law the last few years. More precisely, good teachers point to subjects and rules that have had a change in the *study guide* in the last few years. Where the new edition deviates from recent ones, look to get tested.

This makes sense. If it's an area of change and upheaval, your antennae should be going off. I'll add my own conjecture that the most likely source of such test questions is not a very new rule changed in the newest study guide (the one you must use), but rather in the couple of years before that—especially for the first exam of the year. I say this because LSU's office of testing works with notary test administrators to come up with fair tests, which would seem to require some vetting of and communication on individual questions before they are officially used on the exam. I doubt they have time to use this rigorous procedure for sudden, big changes reflected in the latest edition of the book, at least in the early-year administration. It may be that changes that occurred an edition or two before would be most tested. If you do see a question on the exam that turns on some very recent law, it stands to reason that question is experimental and won't count toward your score. If it's proven to be valid, it will become an official question later. But then it would seem likely that in administrations occurring later in the year, very new changes *would* be ripe for testing.

I would also note the anomaly that, in some years, they may give a January or February exam that allows takers to use either the newest study guide or the one for the previous year. To be fair, this must mean that this first administration, and any exams carried over a week or so later (as they reserve the right to do), will *not* test on changes to the latest study guide. They have to ask questions that could be answered whichever edition is consulted. But the changes captured in the study guide the year *before* all that would be very ripe for testing.

LOUISIANA NOTARY EXAM SIDEPIECE TO THE 2025 STUDY GUIDE

Below are areas of law or the study guide that have changed in the 2025 study guide. Details of the most testable developments from previous years' guides follow (not necessarily the year the law changed). You can anticipate that three to six questions will turn on one of these changes, which should be readily answered if you have indexed the topics well to find the passage that applies. You may also want to go to the text and highlight all new areas of law in a different color from other highlights, or write "NEW" in the margin. That could be a few points that act as low-hanging fruit for you.

The following usually doesn't list the entire page-range for the topic, just the first page. We also don't cover insignificant changes or most of the ones that merely explain in slightly more detail an idea that is already found in earlier editions.

New in the 2025 Study Guide

- 146: new emphasis on how a universal successor may confirm an "absolutely null" donation (such as one not done as authentic act); this is done by authentic act by donor for donations while donor is alive, and even just tacitly by universal successor (through his actions) after donor has died.

- 160: new 2023 case rules that you can't prove compliance with testimonial process and formalities by "extrinsic" evidence (proof outside the actual signed will, such as testimony or affidavits of witnesses). Although the *contents* of a lost or destroyed act may be proved extrinsically (such as an exact photocopy of an already signed act), this doesn't work to prove compliance with form (here, they only had an unsigned copy of the will).

- 162: no clear requirement that an authentic act be dated (unlike a will).

- 173: more on confirmation and ratification that was expanded at p. 146, including explaining difference between the two. Then p. 174 intends to cross-reference p. 146 but has a blank space. These parts *appear* to be inconsistent with each other, but we clear up the ambiguity below, p. 104.

- 177: grounds for dissolving a contract, such as fortuitous event, are just default rules for contracts that may be changed by the contracting parties.

- 199: clarification that default of legal regime applies when couple got married elsewhere; discussion of when Louisiana vs. out-of-state law applies to marital property, which depends on it being movable vs. immovable.

- 208: emphasizes that matrimonial agreement (opting out of the legal regime) is not the same as the contract of marriage (making the couple married), despite similar names. P. 209 expands other terms couples may put in their matrimonial agreement besides choosing the regime, such as dividing up living expenses or pre-determining how alimony would be paid.

- 330: technically, acknowledgment by party only requires that party acknowledge her signature, not sign; but the prudent notary expects it. The next page clarifies that the witness or grantor form *does* require signing.

6 • COMMONLY TESTED CONCEPTS AND MISTAKES

- 446: expanded discussion of what is a "succession" and how it's not a juridical person nor ever owns property. Pp. 447-49 expand on "estate" including different rules based on location of property or decedent's domicile; and if insurance, bank, or investment accounts are part of estate.
- 450: new quotations of code articles on role of succession representative. The next two pages expand on acceptance or renunciation of succession.
- 466: new discussion, and code article, on capacity of interdicted person to make or revoke a will or donation.
- 493: discussion and two recent cases on terms in valid no-contest clauses.
- 564-74: chapter 27 on succession-by-affidavit is greatly expanded and revised, including many changes in the law effective August 2024. It includes (in order): a new emphasis on *gross* value of estate, eligibility where decedent is not domiciled in Louisiana, new rules where decedent had a will but no immovables; repeated discussions of domicile vs. residence and immovables vs. movables, and duties of notary to inquire and advise.

New in the 2024 Study Guide (but page numbers below refer to the 2025 guide)

- 107: new emphasis on how usufructuary may dispose of property damaged or worn out by ordinary use.
- 203: renunciation of right to concur need not be filed, but often is annexed to acts pertaining to that particular community property.
- 333: renewed emphasis that notary to an affidavit is not verifying or attesting to the accuracy or truthfulness of the affiant's statements of fact.
- 424: new emphasis that municipal (street) address must be included in acts affecting immovables; but it isn't actually part of the property description—and isn't enough to satisfy the requirement of a property description (seems testable); new section on "Being that same property" phrasing to refer to a previous description in the public records, to avoid ambiguity.
- 439: where affidavit of correction is for changes to the vehicle title itself, as opposed to other documents, it must be made by both seller and buyer.
- 579: new emphasis that, while a general partnership agreement need not be in English, it must be so if it will be filed with the Secretary of State.

New in the 2023 Study Guide (but page numbers below refer to the 2025 guide)

- 162: new emphasis that a true copy of an AA certified by the same notary is treated as an original, similar to p. 596.
- 428: Revised R.S. 32:705(B) adds three new ways for "endorsement" of a title (new paragraphs (3) through (5)), not requiring a notary. These three methods allow certain transfers to be done without notarization, when: (3) signed over to an insurance company when car is totaled or settled; (4) transferred to/from a licensed dealer; or (5) signed before an 'authorized

officer' for sales involving a secured loan to certain financial institutions. In essence, sales and donations among private parties still need a notary.

- 433: reflecting the above new law, even invoices that used to require a notary no longer do if they fit the circumstances of paragraphs (3)–(5) above.
- 448: Certain accounts pay to beneficiaries outside of succession and are not property of the estate as such, especially IRAs, bank accounts, and life insurance policies. If no beneficiary is named, proceeds are part of estate.
- 449: decedent's body is not property of the estate.
- 472: testator is considered able to read despite eye problems if she can read using mechanical help like magnifying glass; doesn't have to use special procedure and attestation clause for blind testators. Seems testable.
- 481: witness to a testament may be interdicted as long as not really insane, and a mere defect in sight or hearing, short of being blind or deaf, does not disqualify a witness; anyway, such physical infirmity merely affects credibility of witness if called to testify and won't necessarily invalidate the will.
- 516: much-expanded chapter on Trusts includes name ('express' trust) if done by juridical act, and list of purposes to create a trust.
- 518: non-Louisiana trust may be a juridical person, unlike Louisiana trust.
- 520: new sections on trusts for employees (similar to a class trust) and on custodial trusts, including form to create (just in writing).
- 523-24: new sections on life insurance trusts and 'living' trusts—the latter mainly used in common law states. P. 525 adds special needs trusts, which should not be prepared without experience.
- 527: new sections on foreign trusts, real estate investment trusts (REIT), and constructive and resulting trusts (all four are not part of La. trust law).
- 531-33: new and testable section on revocable vs. irrevocable trusts, and difference in revocability between testamentary vs. inter vivos creations.
- 533-35: trustee of private trust must be natural person or a bank or trust company; duties/powers of the trustee, and limits on her delegating them.
- 544: expanded discussion of limits on trust duration, including stipulating excessive term; book mentions common law 'rule against perpetuities.'
- 548: marital portion in trust defined and explained, similar in concept to the forced portion; but this protects a spouse (it applies to successions, too).
- 600-01: new quotation of code articles on presumption of filiation and acknowledgment by AA; revoking acknowledgment (presumably by AA too) by itself doesn't rebut presumption of filiation.

New in the 2022 Study Guide (but page numbers below are for the new guide)

- 87: expanded discussion of immovables by declaration, and new explanation of immovables by destination and by nature; and sometimes animals are immovables too (counterintuitively, so testable).

- 130: clarifies minor's capacity to receive donation (any age) vs. to legally accept one (must be parent or tutor).
- 131-33: expanded examples of donative intent; failure of donation inter vivos may be valid as will; and updated view of donor reserving usufruct.
- 134: clarifies that POA authorizing agent to donate must be express, vs. to *accept* donation need not be.
- 147: even with donation in disguise, the need for *acceptance* still applies.
- 153: clarifies that "obligations" is a broad term: every act made by a notary is an obligation, and notary must learn chapter not just for contracts law.
- 154: new discussions of real obligations, what "heritable" means, & strictly personal obligations; but see inconsistency re "heritable" (below, p. 103).
- 156-57: discusses suspensive, resolutory, and potestative conditions for obligations; contrasts output or requirement contract as not potestative.
- 168: contractual capacity differs from legal capacity (similar to new example of minor receiving donation, p. 130, also noted above).
- 168-73: expanded introductions to, and examples for: capacity, consent, cause, and [certain] object (btw, lawyers call these the 4 C's, a mnemonic).
- 186: new emphasis on recording adult adoption: where, and when effective.
- 254: authorization to *accept* donation must be in writing, but need not be express (can be part of a general authority), nor need it be AA (p. 252).
- 348: notes significant difference (so, test-worthy) between being unable to sign (e.g., incoherent) and having physical difficulty (infirmity, nerves).
- 437: major, oft-tested change in the traditional rule for exempting from odometer statement; previously a car 10 years old+ would be exempt (e.g., a 2011 car would not need it), but now it goes by model year 2010 or older (exempt) vs. a *20*-year delay for model years 2011 or later. This means increasingly cars that used to be exempt now actually need the statement.
- 449: expands discussion of *seizin* and makes clear that succession representative (e.g., executor), once appointed, has capacity to deal with property, even though ownership is immediately vested in successors at death.
- 454: new section on absent (missing) persons who get declared dead, and then pop up, what a colleague of mine calls "the rights of the living dead."
- 469: expanded discussion and examples, several counterintuitive, of sufficient signatures in olographic testaments.

- 478-79: expanded discussion of accretion and joint legacies uses types of legacy (general, particular, universal) to show how accretion works; similarly, p. 480 explains the way to resolve inconsistencies in legacies.
- 484: notes art. 1609 about a revocation of a revocation (=restores will).
- 490: expansion on what happens if an ex-spouse is still in the will—tested!
- 493: discussion of no-contest clauses ("in terrorem") causing forfeiture.
- 496: examples of the "cruel treatment" ground to disinherit.
- 603: expands discussion and new cases on the limits of using act of correction by notary: it's not used to correct substantive errors, and it applies not just to any act (must relate to property).

New in the 2021 Study Guide (but page numbers below are for the new guide)

- 24: expanded mention of process to get certificate of character for notary applications that have issues in that regard.
- 55: new section on notary acting as agent for a party, and how she has no conflict of interest unless she has a "beneficial interest" in the transaction.
- 145: donor who is out of state but donating Louisiana property must abide by Louisiana rules of donation such as authentic act (where that's required); otherwise the donation has no effect here, is void. Seems testable.
- 288: clarifies the difference between general and special mortgages.
- 319: explanation of "imperative" vs. "suppletive" laws.
- 329: list of situations that require more than mere notarization and so either require authentic act or act under private signature duly acknowledged. Seems testable. Note the interaction with the p. 210 material on *when* a matrimonial agreement must be signed. Together that would make a great question, making you look in both places to solve a scenario.
- 336: when caption deviates from content, the content controls; same with incorrect naming of parties in caption or title—seems testable.
- 388: emphasis at item 2 that mortgages require a marital-status-change declaration like many other acts affecting immovables do. Seems testable.
- 483: clarifies that one way to revoke a will is to destroy it; newly sorts out ways to revoke whole will vs. ways to revoke parts of it (only a legacy). Later is a new statement about handwriting on the will itself.
- 500: distinction between designating *who* controls your remains vs. *how* they will be disposed of: the *how* you have no direct control over. Detailed quotation of statutory and military rules on disposition of remains.
- 698: statute on remote online notarization (RON) and related congressional acts: though remote notaries is not mentioned in the text, since it's here in the Appendix it's fair game to test on. The key is to index it.

6 • COMMONLY TESTED CONCEPTS AND MISTAKES

Testable Issues by Subject Matter

Some larger issues are notable for how frequently they are tested, or otherwise are good candidates for coming up on a new test. One can predict, roughly, certain subject areas that deserve more study and cannot be known just vaguely before the exam. This estimate is based on several factors outlined in the next section (where I break down test-worthy issues by chapter, instead of topic), but primarily on what is generally known about recent administrations.

These assumptions should hold true under the new process they may implement in July 2025 or so. If they tested frequently on testaments, for example, that means their pool of tried-and-true questions has a larger number of these questions in it. So a random exam generated from that pool should, statistically, have more such questions than other topics. It's possible, of course, to wind up with few such topics and to face an exam that feels random in covering so many unrelated topics. But until we hear a history otherwise, it's safe to assume these topics will tend to be overrepresented on a random exam, too. This is especially true if they're some of the harder topics and every exam will be assigned a certain number of hard questions, to even out the exam from easier questions.

It's very predictable, for example, that testaments and successions will be tested, as it almost always is. It should be the subject you would study repeatedly, and again the day before the exam. In addition to points of emphasis already noted above in this chapter, especially recent law, here's what I observe to be the *top-10 subjects* ripe for extra study and detailed indexing or cross-referencing:

1. *Testaments and successions, including small successions.* Ch. 24 and 27.

Nearly all the test administrations over the past several years have had an entire section of at least 15 questions on testaments, many including wills-related documents. Not all 15 questions actually tested a rule about wills—examiners can use a wills scenario to jump off to a related question such as property ownership or trusts. But still a dedicated group in the exam was about wills or successions. And questions in other parts of the exam could turn on wills without being labeled as such (such as the heir/legatee difference tested in a question apparently about succession by affidavit). That made for about 20% of the entire exam, some of the harder questions, related to testaments. It's almost as if a notary prep course should spend a fifth of the semester on the subject. They don't, as there's so much else to cover, but self-study should certainly aim for understanding it very well. This is true even as they transition to the new system.

Specific subtopics are discussed in depth in our ch. 10 and 17. Suffice it to say that, beyond the mechanics and definitions of intestate and testate successions, and the formal authentic requirements of a valid will, the examiners may use a scenario to force the candidate to show an understanding of how property is divided up among legatees. And, how the normal process can be changed by a testator (as by disinheriting, or setting up a trust).

The testator may also control the disposition of their remains (through a notarial testament, not an olographic one), p. 500. This subject was tested at least seven times since spring 2019, including a follow-up question on one exam about who gets to make the decision in the event the testator did not specify. The topic was greatly expanded in the 2021 edition of *Fundamentals*. And the 2023 edition added elsewhere (now, p. 449) that a dead body is not really part of the estate.

As for small successions, often called "succession by affidavit" because it's OK to use the procedure for even a large estate if it's old enough, they can readily test the simple math of what's in an estate (in turn making you know what's separate property [our ch. 17], and that the 125k cap is for gross estate value, before debt). They may also test the usual requirement that the testator not have a valid will (if in-state), as well as the more recent exception that allows succession by affidavit in certain testate situations lacking immovable property (p. 566). Small succession was tested three times in 2020, twice in 2023, and twice in 2024. It promises to be a topic of focus in 2025 just because the law changed in 2024.

Also as to small successions, know the heirs that have to sign, or be notified of, the affidavit (or someone with knowledge if only one heir exists and no surviving spouse, p. 568). Don't forget that, when it's in the form of an affidavit, it can't be done by agents under a mandate. That's not intuitive, since absent heirs *are* part of the process—but their interest is satisfied by notice, not a power of attorney. They also occasionally test that small successions are actually found in the Code of Civil Procedure rather than the Civil Code Book III with successions.

2. *Donations*. Ch. 10.

Acts of donations *inter vivos*, especially for immovables or related interests in land, make a good scenario to analyze notarial law, practice, and statutory directives for an authentic act. Information is scattered through the book (not just ch. 10), making it important to index; it's tested enough that you'll also want to review it as a unit, bouncing around in the book.

Topics include: forms of donation (gratuitous, onerous, etc.); form *for* donation (proper construction of the authentic act, if required—and is it?); who may donate, and what; formality and timing of acceptance (in writing, but no longer needing authentic act, and that's *when* donation is effective, p. 134); recordation (p. 152); "magic words" of donative intent (e.g., "I gift," not just "convey" or "transfer," pp. 131-32); different rules for donations of cars (pp. 148, 152, and 434); and ways in which donation *inter vivos* differs from a testament—such as that donations while living can be made via power of attorney (p. 253), but testaments can't be (p. 253).

Note that, although the 2023 study guide placed the distinction between onerous and remunerative donations near the end of the chapter (seemingly an afterthought), in fact it's always been heavily tested—both not needing authentic act to accomplish unless the values are off to the point that it's treated as gratuitous. This was one change in the guide that should not fool anyone into slighting it: *you* should emphasize the different forms of donation and which ones must be authentic. They may test it as a bare question about definitions, or may offer a scenario asking what kind of donation this is: onerous? remunerative? or instead a *dation*? In the process they may test your understanding of the manual gift (p. 148), and the definitional differences between movable and immovable (e.g., car vs. land, see pp. 85-90), and then corporeal vs. incorporeal movables (e.g., car vs. stock shares, pp. 85, 88, 148-49). Even within incorporeal movables, rules differ if it's evidenced by a certificate or instrument.

Proper construction and content of the act of donation is very important, but it's found at pp. 383-86, not ch. 10—so, index that subtopic, and cross-reference to it from ch. 10 in a few places. And no example form is given. The subject is tested enough that it's worth the effort to write a sample act somewhere in the book and index to that completed form. At least, study a completed donation, such as the one below in our ch. 18.

All four exams in 2019 had extensive questions or a whole library on donation *inter vivos* (and two of these had a fairly extensive *dation* element in it). Donations have been tested at least 13 times since then, and *dation* often as well.

3. *Other transfers and ownership of property, especially immovables, and related instruments such as mortgages and usufruct.* Ch. 9, 18, 21 and 23.

Beyond donations, transfers of immovables are done through sale or exchange. Forms of transfer include: cash sale, credit sale, exchange, quitclaim, sale with right of redemption, *dation*, and timber sales. They seem to test, repeatedly, an ability to identify which version it is from seeing a library excerpt or from "magic words" in the scenario (e.g., a credit sale often has language of "vendor's privilege," "vendor's lien," or "owner-financed," p. 370). All of these forms have specific content and terms in their acts, detailed in the study guide, and may have "additional provisions for conveyances" (so, cross-reference a lot to p. 386). The concept of bond-for-deed seems to get frequent one-off questions—oddly, because it really isn't a property transfer at all (p. 373). And increasingly they seem to test on partitions.

And beyond transfers of interests in land, there's what *kind* of property interest it may be. A recurring area to test—with several exams asking multiple questions—is the very-civil-law concept of usufruct and naked ownership (ch. 9, but it also arises in aspects of several other chapters, such as the usufruct of a surviving spouse in ch. 24 [see our ch. 17 below]). Usufructs were repeatedly tested in 2022 and 2024.

Related to transfers of immovables are instruments secondary to their sale or conveyance, especially mortgages including collateral mortgages, and accompanying documents such as the promissory note. They used to test collateral mortgages a lot, but I get the impression it's not as heavily tested recently as it used to be (though it was on one fall 2020 exam, and at least once since then). Yet it's still important to learn all such documents that accompany a sale of an immovable and their differences in terms of who must sign; whether it's recorded, and where; whether it's a negotiable instrument (and their relation to UCC9 security agreements); and whether it requires a paraph by the notary. It's crucial to keep straight all the parties to such a transaction, because now there's a lender who is also a "mortgagee."

A related testable area: which situations require, in the appearance, part of a social security number? It's important to write out such a list somewhere in the book and then index to it (gathered from the guide's scattered examples). See below, at ch. 15, for a complete list and suggested place to annotate your book.

Transfers of interests in *movables* may also be tested, such as questions based on ch. 23 about titled vehicles. They don't have the extensive notarial forms, and detailed content, that acts for immovables do. But OMV has its own quirky rules about the certificate of title, donations, and even what a name is (no apostrophes, no Sr., no spaces (p. 441). So, Le Fleur is entered as LEFLEUR. Even St. Andalone would, technically, be STANDALONE, worth remembering as a guide.

4. *Trusts*. Ch. 25.

It's easy to embed some trust questions into a scenario that appears to be about property or successions. E.g., a library document can include part of a will that creates a trust, or tries to. A property section can have a question or two on what-if-it's-a-trust. Recent topics have included: pet trusts (p. 525); who can serve as trustee (p. 533, including some juridical persons); whether a trust is a juridical person (*no*, if a Louisiana trust, p. 517, unlike other states); the settlor as beneficiary (pp. 517, 538); and who owns the property under a trust (the trustee, unlike in common law states, p. 517).

The 2023 study guide greatly expanded the Trusts chapter, and the June 2024 exam had a large number of questions on trusts or related (like using a power of attorney in it). The newer material details several "new" types of trusts, targeted for specific situations like employees or special needs. Although the text advises only an experienced notary should work on these types, their definitions and rules are fair game for testing. Nonetheless, it is doubtful that going forward they will repeat the theme of the June 2024 exam, and instead questions on trusts will likely be scattered and based on scenarios rather than a document. This is especially true once the exam moves to a random on-screen exam, because the pool of trust questions doesn't seem to match the June 2024 emphasis.

5. *Appointment and regulation of notaries*. Ch. 7 and Appendix A.

This kind of background information (even "trivia") was a major part of the exam when part of it was closed book and tested "general knowledge." You'd get the idea from reading the SOS website that this section is abandoned, as if all questions now draw on a library or involve a scenario. Not so. The closed-book aspect is gone, but most exams seem to have about 10 questions that may be called a "legacy" of the old format, now spread among other parts. One can guess they would split these between "notarial practice" and, less so, our #7 below on the civil law system. Know who appoints a notary (the Governor); eligibility for appointment (e.g., valid voter, no felons unless pardoned); their duties; who disciplines them; and for what. Notary practice includes the fact that a commission is parish-based (vs. statewide *jurisdiction*, tested September 2024), the "de facto doctrine" (p. 69); duties of recordation (ch. 6, 7); and statutory directives in acts (pp. 62-63). But the "practice of law" is forbidden (pp. 76-79, 321). It's tempting to gloss over the early chapters as mere set-up to the heart of the study guide, when in reality several questions may test the back-stories in our items #5 and #7.

6. *Recordation of documents*. Various chapters, as specified in our Index below.

The exam may be peppered with isolated questions (or parts of the A-D choices) that turn on requirements for recording a specific act—who does it, when, and where. These details would be hard to memorize but fortunately can be indexed well (see our ch. 12 under "R") and answered the day of the exam. If a question turns on whether and where a specific instrument is filed for registry, as for example the adult adoption tested recently (it must be, but any parish's clerk of court will do, pp. 186, 603), you should be able to find the recording rules somewhere it's discussed (in this instance, both places, but often it's in only one of the two or three guide sections on a topic). Many miscellaneous topics raise additional recording issues, and the examiners do seem to come back to that aspect.

The examiners tend to test the notary's different time period to record acts involving immovables depending on whether the property is located in Orleans Parish (48 hours) vs. all other parishes (15 days), p. 59. But note that the act can stipulate that the notary instead deliver the instrument to the parties or otherwise refrain from filing, relieving the notary of the duty, p. 60.

7. *Louisiana civil law tradition and organization of code law*. Ch. 2-5.

As with notarial practice, above, the legacy of general knowledge seems here to stay even if it's not emphasized in the SOS website. This may include: how the common law differs (e.g., civil law's supremacy of the legislature vs. judge-made law); structure of the court system; what "law" is just advisory (Attorney General opinions, and to some extent even court decisions); and origins of our civil code (especially its distinction from "Napoleonic Code"). They even test—maybe one question?—*where* in the statutes certain law will be found (e.g., notary law is in Title 35; small successions in the Code of Civil Procedure), which would be hard if you had not indexed subjects beyond what the glossary offers.

Besides the several introductory chapters, areas of substantive law later in the book (matrimonial regimes, lease, security agreements, corporate forms, etc.) seem ideal for several miscellaneous questions, but would be quickly answered if you index the study guide and can find the specifics. All told, such legacy questions and other standalone ones (devoted to specifics not tied to a scenario) may comprise some 10 questions of about 55. You simply cannot skip reading the introductory chapters closely, and indexing areas of substantive law later in the book, even areas inapt for a scenario. Grab the miscellaneous low-hanging fruit.

8. *Power of attorney*. Ch. 15.

Although you must know the difference between procuration and mandate (the former is unilateral—the agent need not sign), in reality they are two flavors of the same instrument: *power of attorney*. This is not about "attorneys" at all, rather it delegates—from principal to agent—the power to act on behalf of the principal who makes it. The agent can be called an attorney-in-fact, because of their power to act legally or sign legal documents for someone else, but it's not the unauthorized practice of law. (Agent is also called a mandatary or representative, depending on whether it happens to come under a mandate or procuration.)

The document creating this relationship, using the common law term that the study guide makes clear is fine for these purposes, is the power of attorney (POA). It's used in simple business deals, as when a real estate agent acts on your behalf to make an offer, or when you authorize GEICO to sign your car title as part of the totaling of your wrecked car. Or it can be used in complex and emotional family issues (letting someone make medical decisions for you, then called a medical mandate or health care power of attorney), or more complex business decisions, as when all siblings delegate to one of them the power to deal with and eventually donate the family home they've inherited together. The POA is so commonly tested that you may want to look over the sample in our ch. 18.

Louisiana POAs, unlike in many other states, are by default "durable" (p. 260), i.e., the contract and the agent's power continue even if the principal gets incapacitated. (The original act could always make it non-durable.) Of course, one main reason to sign a POA is to allow the agent to act in the event of a disability.

In the family situation, the main thing they test is the conditional procuration (p. 251), in which medical and business decisions are invested in the agent, but only *after* a condition of disability happens to the principal. You have to know not only how the original power of attorney is properly drafted, plus how to create an act that triggers the delegation—to declare the disability exists. That is established following a specific process (with either one doctor or two certifying it, turning on how the original procuration was worded), and it's an authentic act.

Another testable subject, for POAs even without a condition to trigger it (most of them do take effect immediately), is the requirement that the agent's powers be specified and not generally stated. For the agent to be able to transfer land, the POA must say so (p. 253). The book stresses that the power to *donate* must be spelled out; just authorizing "transfers" doesn't empower donation (p. 254). Similarly, a "general" POA that doesn't specify medical decisions isn't treated as a medical mandate.

Finally, they test whether a POA must be an authentic act. Technically, "no," so it can be informal (the mandate version, as a contract between two people, doesn't even have to be in writing, but it usually is for any serious transaction besides agreeing to buy a scratch-off together). *BUT* the agent's power to act is limited by the form of the original empowerment: they can only do what the POA instrument allows them to do. This is not the rule, above, of what has to be specified in the POA, but really its *form* (p. 252). If not in writing, it doesn't allow the agent to do something that requires a writing, like taking out a mortgage. If not in authentic form, the agency is limited to doing acts that themselves don't require authentic form. For example, donation of immovables is an authentic act, so the POA empowering it must be authentic, too; same with a POA used to sign, for someone else, a mortgage using a confession-of-judgment clause.

For this reason, in practice many POAs are both authentic and specific, giving the agent broad authority. They may test you with a POA that would work just fine for a decision, like many medical ones, that don't have to be done via authentic act—but it fails as a device to allow the agent to do something listed among the many acts requiring authentic form (pp. 326-27). This is especially testable because it requires you to know this rule about the form of POAs *and* which acts are authentic, making you look in two places of the guide.

A list of the things one cannot do via POA is in our ch. 15. Chief among them are making testaments and affidavits, since donating after death and swearing an oath are *personal* acts. This means that even a POA in authentic form purporting to delegate will-making to a relative doesn't actually permit that.

9. *Miscellaneous family law issues*. Ch. 12, 24, and 29.

They seem to pick one area of legal change to a family situation and ask questions about it related to a different topic, such as wills or property. Examples ripe for testing include: limited emancipation; tutorship by will; temporary authority to make medical and school decisions for a minor; acknowledgment of paternity; and adult adoption. Emancipation and adoption probably get tested the most.

Most such contexts have a discussion about the law in one place in the book, then a form to accomplish it elsewhere (often in ch. 29), as with tutorship (pp. 188 and 615). The two places repeat a lot of the same information, but there may be some aspect that is on one page but not the other (such as recordation rules). Each subject is fully covered if you write page-specific cross-references (see our ch. 13, below, with detailed page references to insert into each place) or you index all places (ch. 12). Knowing just one of the two or three places where the issue is handled won't be enough on game day, as you can't count on one discussion being enough to answer their question. In fact, you should study the areas that don't overlap, because you can guess that's what they'll test.

10. *Clauses in juridical acts*. Ch. 19.

Overlapping with many of the subjects above (such as wills, transfers, and donations), it's important to know the particular phrases and clauses used for specific acts. They vary by context, as ch. 19 lays out. For example, the *conclusions* of authentic acts vs. testaments vs. affidavits are distinctive and testable. An entire section of *two* 2022 exams (and once in 2023) tested the appropriate appearance clause and other apt phrasings by context, and was considered difficult. The key is to read ch. 19 repeatedly, add cross-references in it, and be ready to find the applicable clauses or identifying language under time pressure. We explain the big picture on these acts and components in ch. 7-11.

It also helps, as suggested in ch. 14 below, to use some of the blank pages to write out a few samples of acts in various contexts (e.g., donation and affidavit). This way you learn-by-doing not only the general structure and components of such acts but also the unique clauses you use for that specific act.

10A? *Property descriptions?* Ch. 22.

Though it'd make sense to include this in the top-10, and the chapter must be read, it's a strategic question whether knowing it inside and out will pay off for the exam. There have been nightmare administrations in the early 2010s that featured several difficult questions (and had low pass rates), and some of the 2018 exams had multiple questions on the subject. Lately, for most exams, it seems to be a couple miscellaneous questions if tested at all. Most exams have had practically none, other than recognizing what to do with property straddling parishes—more about filing; others had two or three questions at most, and they were more definitional and straightforward than difficult math examples of "metes and bounds."

Decoding every nuance of ch. 22 may take enormous time spent on other matters more testable and certainly more used in practice—it'd be malpractice for you to create a property description from scratch as part of a land transfer! But certainly some exams since 2020 have included a couple questions. Typically, when there is one, it's easier than you'd expect, like identifying the form of description (labeling it by comparing to examples in the book).

At the least, learn the actual examples the study guide gives, e.g., how to read a 36-square section, p. 404. And generally know the terms such as metes and bounds, p. 408, as opposed to describing by sections or by subdivisions, p. 411, the latter being easier—or the *per aversionem* form, p. 407, which was tested for its simple definition once in 2020 and again in 2024.

Most likely, they'd test descriptions in relation to other subjects, such as recordation—where the question looks like it's about the description but is answered by a different chapter in the book, wasting the time of someone stuck in ch. 22. They certainly test regularly on *when* a property description is needed in an instrument (not just an address), which is noted throughout ch. 21 for each type of property transfer.

Additional Testable Issues by Chapter

Within each chapter, or for each subject matter, there seem to be a few notable topics that are ripe for testing. This is simply my best estimate, based on: emphases in the study guide (look for rules or case law repeated in two or more places in the book, or for topics where it says something like "a good notary would know..."); information from the last seven years' exams; hints in the old

6 • COMMONLY TESTED CONCEPTS AND MISTAKES

exam questions at the end of other recent guides; and topics that make for difficult but fair testing based on my own test-writing experience.

It's not some "inside baseball" from the examiners themselves. Still, in each chapter, there has to be an emphasis on knowing cold these specific subtopics, or at least being able to find details about them during the exam. Here's a list of possibly emphasized topics for each chapter, not to the exclusion of other topics.

The following is largely *in addition to* the topics already noted above in this chapter under other headings, such as the top issues by subject matter. The following may not be in the top 10—or weren't covered above otherwise—but they deserve your attention. The digit to the left represents a chapter number.

1. notary as public official • importance of the authentic act and record-keeping

2. civil law judges only interpret the law • legislature is supreme law-maker

3. Louisiana notaries have more powers and responsibilities than common law ones • in this sense notaries are professionals and more than "official witnesses"

4. authority to revoke or suspend commission for cause rests with the courts • specifically the level of court most involved with such matters is the District Court, since that's where a rule to show cause would be filed by the DA or AG (p. 665)

5. general organization ("books") of the Civil Code • meaning of "jurisprudence"

6. Clerk of Court is "parish recorder" • list of notarial instruments recorded with Clerk of Court (p. 42)

7. official misconduct, including misfeasance and malfeasance • injuring public records • notary's powers listed by R.S. 35:2 • duty to record • liability of notary

8. corporeal, incorporeal, movable, immovable • fruits • acquisitive prescription

9. usufruct: fruits, termination, divisibility, inventory • predial servitude: negative, affirmative, apparent, nonapparent • usufructuary cannot create predial

10. list of prohibited donations (pp. 137-42) • four exceptions to requirement of authentic act • acceptance: who, how, when • irrevocability and exceptions (split across pp. 132-33 and 142) • compare and contrast donation *mortis causa* (will)

11. obligations is broader than contracts • types of contracts, list (pp. 167-68) • four C's of contract formation • "cause" is *not* "consideration" • nullity

12. domicile • tutorship • matrimonial regimes and agreements • fruits of SP=CP

13. things that may be sold, including a hope • ambiguities interpreted against seller • warranty of peaceful possession • lesion (only by seller, only if immovable)

14. lease requires: thing, rent, term • recording lease • transfer of ownership

15. ways to terminate a mandate (p. 260) • completion after principal dies

16. three kinds of suretyship • guarantor is not a joint debtor in true suretyship

17. two ways pledge still exists • largely replaced by UCC9 security agreements • perfection of a security interest

18. property that may be mortgaged • recording a mortgage • cancellation • documents as part of collateral mortgage package • recording collateral mortgages

19. see ch. 8, 9, and 11 below, discussing in detail these much-tested notarial acts; see ch. 7 below, on affidavits and verification of pleadings

20. oaths are personal, so they can't be done under POA or by acknowledgment

21. vendor's lien or privilege • quitclaim deed • additional provisions for conveyances (p. 386) • content of mortgage • executory process • counterletters • NPI

22. forms of property description • finding a numbered section • describing one • following a metes and bounds description from commencing point • boundaries

23. odometer disclosure statements and when not required • affidavit of heirship • act of correction on certificate of title • sales and use tax • rescinded sales

24. see our ch. 10 and 17, below, on notarial testaments, authentic form, separate property, and successions

25. creating trusts • who may be settlor, trustee, and beneficiary • recordation • use of trust principal for income beneficiary • forced portion in trust • refusals

26. reporting directly to court via certified copy of procès verbal • recapitulation is a summary

27. see ch. 10 and 17, below, on small successions (a/k/a succession by affidavit)

28. assumed business name (vs. trade name) only applies to sole proprietorship, LLC, and partnership, not a corp • articles of incorporation: content and filing

29. act of correction (two versions) • limits on "true copy" by notary, and certifying birth certificates • tutorship by will • act of partition • limited emancipation • provisional custody by mandate

30. alternatives to personal appearance by all parties • confirmation of imperfect donation, to cure it • disclaimers, "attesting to signature only" • non-English acts

Common Mistakes to Avoid

Some typical errors are easily made but can be avoided by being aware and double-checking oneself. Don't give up free points by doing this:

1. *Definitional mix-ups.* One or two questions may actually turn on terminology trivia, such as remembering that "legatee," not "heir," fits with testate successions. I say "trivia" because in law practice it wouldn't matter much if you talked about an inheritor being an "heir" even though really they take under a will. But on the exam...! The start of this chapter has a list of many definitional twisters.

2. *Mixing up parties or roles in scenario.* They may use confusing names and relationships which are easy to blend under exam pressure. You may need to make a few notes in the scenario to keep straight who's who. They may test parties not by actual names like Cathy but your understanding of role terms like mortgagee, legatee, and attorney in fact.

3. *Mixing up parties acting <u>in a role</u> in a scenario.* Meaning, they may be acting in a representative capacity rather than individually. It is no minor thing to keep straight which role they're acting in. Sometimes the same-named person acts for herself *and* in her role as agent, trustee, LLC member, or similar capacity, as for example "Martha" does in a sample scenario, p. 734. They're also big on knowing appearance clauses for people acting in such a capacity, as in pp. 357-59 of ch. 19. Specifically, you could remember to name the principal first, and all that appearance info in detail before introducing the agent (p. 338), by associating the word "principal" with "first": of *course* the principal goes first. You'll also be expected to figure out the proper signature line for such a person, e.g., "John Deaux, by and through agent, Amber Dextris."

4. *Mixing up the "negative" of a question.* The format may ask which of the following statements is false (or ask what's prohibited). It's easy in an exam situation to think you're answering correctly when that's the option they meant for you to *eliminate*. See p. 16 above about a method during the test to not trick yourself this way. Committing to marking the question up in this way may save a point or two just because the wording of the question is hard to follow or may be a double negative.

5. *Mixing up rules for intestate and testate successions.* For example, only testate situations raise issues of forced heirship and disinheriting someone; and small-successions eligibility may turn on the presence of a will. An olographic will can't provide for disposition of remains (p. 500), and can't be signed with just a mark (p. 348). During the exam it's hard to keep the situations straight. Don't go only by memory; confirm any answer you're giving by locating it in the part of ch. 24 you should be on, for that scenario.

6. *Mixing up types of servitudes.* Usufruct is a *personal* servitude and is commonly tested. It's not the same as an encumbrance on the property itself because of the relationship between two tracts (*predial*), where you're focused on the dominant and servient estates (p. 113). Even within personal servitudes, there may be a question that sorts out usufruct vs. right of habitation vs. right of use (though usufruct is the most tested). These three are similar but you'll need to be able to find the key differences on exam day (such as that right of use is fully heritable and transferable, p. 112). And it's easy to confuse right of "passage" or

"way," which is a predial servitude (p. 116), with right of "use," which is personal. Indexing the terms may fix that.

7. *Counterintuitive words.* It's easy to test your (mis)understanding of definitions, as part of a larger question, when the words don't mean what they sound like. Look for these along the way and make a mental note that something's funky about the word. Examples: "private things" like cop cars can still be owned by the government, p. 84, not just "public things"; "vulgar" substitutions are actually OK, it's the regular ones that may be forbidden, p. 486; and "legal" may mean done automatically by operation of law, not by a judge (a "judicial" act), so it's not the opposite of "illegal" (e.g., legal servitude, p. 115).

Also, "confusion" is a term of art for when the same person obtains both the dominant and servient estates (extinguishing the servitude, p. 126), and is sort of the opposite of "destination of the owner," p. 120. An "ordinary suretyship" is actually an uncommon form, p. 267. "Real right" is not really a right in real estate or real property, p. 273. The procès verbal is actually a written report, p. 553.

Some "donations" are not really acts of giving (more like contracts or repayments), so they aren't treated as donations and don't need authentic acts. Some "sales" are such unfair exchanges, like a mansion for $1000, that it's not a sale but a "donation in disguise," p. 147, needing authentic form.

And, famously, naked owners may be fully clothed....

8. *Omitting formalities of or parties to an authentic act.* Many of the book's many "caveat notarius" [watch out] warnings relate to a failure to use or formalize the required indicators of authentic form, such as order of signing, or actual presence of witnesses (e.g., pp. 637-42). It's such a recurring theme that they're signaling it'll be tested, and likely on more than one question.

Further common errors made in analyzing authentic acts, in particular, are discussed below at the end of ch. 8.

7

The Four <u>A</u>'s of Notarial Functions

Chapter 19 of the study guide is the most important (if not the wills chapter, 24). It's dense, and worth reading several times. It isn't easy to follow, as there's some repetition and disorganization with topics that are introduced in a fairly lengthy way, then explained and illustrated more, later in the chapter. The most obvious culprit is the long discussion of appearance clauses in pp. 338-43, including some sample language to use in an act—and then pp. 357-59 have even more sample forms, with examples of phrases for "appearing" in various capacities (as an agent, as a member of an LLC, as a spouse, etc.). Pay attention to cross-references *within* ch. 19 so that you'll know, on test day, to look in another spot for the example on-point to your question.

Another confusing thing about ch. 19 is that it splits information about affidavits across three places in the chapter (as clarified in our ch. 13 cross-references to add, on the affidavit and its component parts). I don't think affidavits belong in this chapter. It certainly is a "juridical act," so it should be mentioned as an example fitting the chapter title, but it's different enough from authentic acts (ch. 19's main topic) that it'd be clearer to sort it out and give it one section, or better yet, its own chapter. And certainly the component list for authentic acts should not mention parts of affidavits on it like "evidence of oath" (so, our next chapter gives a less confusing list of the parts of an authentic act). I mean, the notarial testament is also a "juridical act," but it gets its own chapter.

The main downside to ch. 19 is that it's so informatively dense, right from the start, that the authors never quite step back and explain why they break down various notarial acts the way they do, and how they relate to other important instruments covered in other chapters, especially testaments.

This part of our book seeks to provide a bigger picture, to conceptualize the main functions of a notary. The next chapter conceptualizes, and gives structure to, the *authentic act* in particular.

There are certainly more than four functions that notaries perform in Louisiana. P. 55 spells out all the legitimate roles notaries play. The examiners do test that you recognize these broader functions, such as conducting family meetings, administering oaths (statewide, even for notaries with jurisdiction in limited parishes, as many have if they were commissioned before 2005), and managing inventories of estates (ch. 26). Notaries don't just do *four* things.

Still, the four *primary* functions, stated here in terms of the four main actions notaries perform, permeate the exam—and set up all the details of how they differ, readily tested (such as that many authentic acts can be done via an agent, while affidavits cannot). Your conceptual organization may vary and work fine, but I believe the easiest and most memorable way to organize most of what notaries do in practice—and what's most tested on the exam—is to think of these functions as *the four A's*. I've chosen an order to dispense with the two easiest functions first, with the first one found outside ch. 19 of the study guide but closely related to the notarial acts detailed in that chapter.

1. ATTESTING TO SIGNATURES

The most basic function notaries perform is to identify a signer, watch them sign, and verify by the notary's seal (signature) that this person did sign this document. This works with forms that the notary has created and, often, with standardized forms the customer brings to the process. This attestation function is the one shared with common law notaries, who do have at least this very important role in commerce or public administration (if little else).

The main things tested about attestation are (1) the acceptable identifications or substitutes for ID allowed in the process of verifying who is signing (study guide pp. 74, 337), and (2) the ethical and practical necessity of making sure the right person signs, and does that in front of the notary. They may try to get you to regard some imperfect procedure as good enough, when it is not, such as the cautionary tale on pp. 74-75 about having one signer vouch for the second signer's identity when neither signer is personally known to the notary.

These questions should be low-hanging fruit on the exam if you keep in mind that the easy way to comply is simply to do what you've sworn on the form that you've done: verify the person and watch them sign. They may also test whether the person is signing in the correct capacity (e.g., as an individual on one part of a form, but as an agent for another elsewhere on the form, as seen on a sample question at study guide p. 734). Finally, keep in mind that a mandatary or other agent signs their own name to the form, and is the one identified for attestation, rather than having the principal's named "forged" onto the signature line (below, p. 131).

2. AFFIDAVITS

Notaries administer oaths, such as by swearing in a witness before a deposition or certifying an oath of office (as will be done for you when you take the oath before finalizing your commission with the SOS). One step beyond giving the oath is drafting and notarizing the *affidavit*, which is a fancy way of saying someone's written statement of fact made under oath.

Up front, note that the information about, and component parts of, affidavits are inexplicably split across pp. 333, 343, 345, and 361 in ch. 19, and a part repeated at p. 616. The authors used to place it all together in ch. 20, which to me made more sense. I guess they now want to relate the affidavit to other notarial acts in ch. 19—but it's the *differences* that matter more, and there's no reason to cover it piecemeal throughout an already complicated chapter.

7 ▪ FOUR A's OF NOTARIAL FUNCTIONS

It *is* conceptually accurate to see a properly drafted affidavit as similar to the framework and content of other notarial acts such as the authentic act. Many of the elements overlap, such as preamble, appearance clause, and conclusion. But the purpose and structure is just different enough, and easy enough to learn on its own, that it's best to see it as its own animal rather than a variation of other notarial acts like the authentic act. Nonetheless, at bottom the affidavit is an act—a unilateral juridical act (see p. 333)—made by the "affiant" (the one swearing to facts), with magic words such as the "jurat" (p. 616) to make it tick.

By "unilateral," the study guide simply means that it's not a group ritual the way most authentic acts and most contracts are. It's just one person saying X is true, in front of a public officer swearing them in and verifying they read and signed it—swore to it in writing. It's so unilateral that the notary is *not independently verifying the accuracy* of the statements made by the affiant. Presumably the notary is acting properly to prepare and notarize a statement by the affiant that the affiant is divorced (which turns out not to be true) or drives a Mercedes (he in fact rides a Vespa). At the least there is no independent duty to investigate the facts sworn to, though there is some general duty of the notary to verify the competence of signers and actors in a transaction (see pp. 320 and 503-04).

By "juridical," the book simply means "legal" (i.e., relating to law or having legal consequences), not that it be done by a judge or in court. In fact, affidavits and many other juridical acts are usually made out-of-court. Much of the point of affidavits and authenticated proof is to avoid having to establish the issue during a trial, if at all possible.

The *magic words* of an affidavit that certainly separate it from other notarial acts is the "jurat," meaning the phrase: "Sworn to and subscribed before me this ___ day of _____, 20___," and sometimes adding the city and state of signing (examples in study guide at pp. 361, 440, and 616, and below, ch. 18). The term *jurat* may be tested, and certainly the requirement of the phrase is highly testable. A proper affidavit will have a jurat in its conclusion, while a different magic phrase is used for *other* acts, such as "Thus done and passed..." (p. 345). You know it's purporting to be an affidavit (or at least a variation like "verification of pleadings") when you see the jurat; and even some very different acts (such as a small succession affidavit) may use such an attestation in closing.

Most examples of affidavits given in the study guide are presented in the third person: the affiant as speaker but the notary as narrator. The affiant appears before the notary ("me") and swears to facts from the point of view of the memorializer of the statement, the notary, who repeats the statement in the third person ("that he is a resident of Caddo Parish"; "that she sold the car on March 7, 2022"; "that he was married but once, to Mary Smith").

In actual practice, affidavits may have the affiant tell her own story in the first person ("I am a resident of Caddo Parish," etc.). But one clear difference between an affidavit and a testament, for exam purposes, is that the testament is in the first person (the testator says "I") while the affidavit doesn't have to be, except for the introductory and conclusional contributions in the *notary's* voice. Remember that the notary is the one administering the oath, and the affiant's voice or content is contained within that shell. The formal parts are the notary's.

Even before the all-important closing lines (jurat with date, followed by notary's signature), the other distinctive feature of an affidavit is its "evidence of oath" near the beginning, before the core statements which the affiant is making. Here, you're expected to know that an affiant "appears" before the notary (often in a briefer appearance clause than one would expect for an authentic act), who verifies that an oath was administered and the content is about to follow. Typically the evidence of oath is the phrase: "Who, after being duly sworn, did depose and say...."

The exact structure and order of a valid affidavit is set out on p. 334 of the study guide. There, on the provided list near the end of the page, go ahead and write the language of a jurat ("Sworn to and subscribed before me...") so you don't have to flip to another page to quote it. I don't know why the book's "Components" list puts the "date" bulletpoint where they do, since it's typically *after* the signature and part of the jurat. Anyway, the jurat's phrasing is included on p. 345 and explained at p. 616. You'll use it a lot in practice, even outside the context of formal affidavits (see our p. 129 below).

Also, go ahead and write "evidence of oath" next to that third bullet on p. 334. It would've been helpful if they'd labeled it for you and referenced p. 343.

Our ch. 18 has examples of actual affidavits, annotated. You may want to write one, or a similar complete sample of an affidavit (not just a list of parts), onto a blank page somewhere handy (or p. 361), and cross-reference to it from p. 333.

Also, at those spots, you should write a cross-reference to the affidavit's close cousin the "verification of pleadings." It's in a whole other chapter, at p. 633.

In civil procedure nowadays, there's not as many uses for a verification of pleadings as there used to be, when all sorts of statements accompanying a lawsuit's filing had to be "verified" (notarized) and not just signed: procedure is streamlined now to make it less common. But for exam purposes you just need to know the notary's role in verifying pleadings, not the contexts that still require it. And in practice you will still get a regular number asking you to notarize a verification, so it's right to be included in the study guide.

A verification of pleadings is essentially an affidavit swearing that the petition's assertions of fact are true. And a "verification of interrogatories" does the same thing for answers to discovery requests the other side in litigation has asked. The notary doesn't affirm their truth (just like with an affidavit), just that the signer affirms them. Verifying pleadings is not the practice of law—as would be drafting pleadings or advising about them (p. 321).

3. "AUTHENTIC ACT" (INSTRUMENTS IN "AUTHENTIC FORM")

This is by far the most tested form of notarial instrument, especially when you consider that many other things they test on, such as donations and certain mortgages, are forms of the authentic act. It is covered in ch. 19, as a general matter, and specific examples are found in many places throughout the study guide. You'll have an index of all the acts that must be in authentic form by expanding pp. 326-27, as suggested below in ch. 9. Our own list there expands on the entries already in your guide, and adds more page references.

The concept and structure of the authentic act is our next chapter. The one after that shares all the instances in which authentic acts are required, followed by a chapter of some tips on the specific application of the notarial testament, which is closely related to the authentic act. Ch. 17 expands further on the concept behind wills and successions, allowing this difficult subject—which cuts across several chapters in the study guide—to be harnessed and answered on the exam.

4. ACKNOWLEDGED ACT

This is the poor stepchild of the authentic act. But it has some real uses in practice where not all the parties can come before a notary, or two competent witnesses are not, or were not, present. It's covered in ch. 11 below.

8

Concept and Structure of the Authentic Act

It's an Event, and You're Emcee and Narrator

Think of the authentic act as not just a document or legal instrument that accomplishes some goal. Think of it as an "act" in the sense of an *action*. It's an event. The document memorializes that event, but the event itself is important and has characteristics of its own, apart from the document produced from it. You know that a wedding is a ceremony, not just a bunch of signed forms. The authentic act isn't quite to that level of ritual and planning, but think of it along those lines, with the notary officiating.

The notary, in an authentic act, is not just an attester of signatures to a complex document. And not just a scribe to someone else's facts (as with the affidavit). Instead, the notary is the emcee to an event—a literal master of ceremonies. In the process the notary is also the narrator and memorializer of the event. The document that results is not so much a *product* of the event as it is a play-by-play *narration* of it. Once you understand that this is more than a signing ceremony (though it is that, too), all the ritual and formal requirements of an authentic act make sense. It is certainly a role for the civil law notary unlike anything found in the common law—where a notary would commit the unauthorized practice of law by acting as an active participant (or worse, document drafter) in the legal procedure at hand.

Notaries in Louisiana cannot practice law, either (stressed at study guide pp. 76-79 and 564, and certainly testable). But many aspects of a notary's role in overseeing legal instruments are not *defined* here as the "practice of law," if a notary does it without giving legal advice. While in Kentucky or Kansas, say, creating a will for someone even without offering legal advice (even just memorializing the wishes of the testator) could be a crime! So the same prohibition—don't "practice law" unless you're a lawyer—is true in all states. But Louisiana deviates greatly in allowing the notary a substantive, independent role in the authentic act.

Given that notaries here may officiate at authentic acts (oversee the event, draft the document), and that many types of legal actions can only be taken via authentic acts (see our next chapter), the notary exam heavily tests all aspects of this event and document. Understanding the concept of the act and the notary's emcee/narrator's role at the meeting that takes place makes it more intuitive to see how such acts are structured and how the ritual must be performed.

All authentic acts share a similar structure, that should be written somewhere accessible in the book. The guide shows the structure for an affidavit on p. 334, but somehow omits a similar bulletpoint for the more-tested authentic act (the list below that on p. 335 is too generic, for "juridical acts"). I set it out below in bold, with some explanatory notes you could write in or shorten. A good place to write it is on the last blank page of the guide (facing the inside back cover), leaving room to add all sorts of notes, phrasings, examples you'd like to have handy as you construct such an act. Use page numbers to make the framework a mini-index, too. Our ch. 18 offers an example of an authentic act, annotated.

The structure below makes sense if you think of the authentic act as a *story* told by the notary about an event. After the *title*, and setting of *location* (venue), the notary *introduces* himself or herself (introduction), then *welcomes* in the key players (appearances), describes the main *action* of the plot (body of act), then *winds up* the tale (conclusion). Once everybody *signs off* on it in the proper order, the script is done.

Thinking of it as a story with characters who appear at different times also helps you to remember the order in which they must sign, which is testable (and should be written somewhere handy as a reminder, such as top of p. 326; see next chapter). The *order of signing* is always:

parties → 2 witnesses → notary

Drafting Authentic Acts and Structure: Write into Study Guide

- **Title** (Heading or Caption), e.g., "Act of Usufruct" or "Limited Emancipation by Authentic Act"
- **Venue** (or can precede Title): "it's where your feet are" is the catchy reminder by Shane Milazzo—meaning it's where it's *signed* that counts
- **Introduction** (Preamble): establishes the capacity of the Notary
- **Appearance Clause(s)**: important *and testable* introduction of the party or parties to the act
- **Body of Act** (core): the law provides the defining *substance or content* of the act
- **Conclusion** (starts "Thus done and passed..." or similar): ties it together
- **Signatures** of party, witnesses, and notary (and recent statutory requirements: printed or typed names under signing; notary ID #)

Common Mistakes with the Authentic Act

They often test you by giving you a scenario or part of a library document that deviates, in some crucial (or even minor but technically important) way, from the required components, details, or formalities of a valid authentic act. Our ch. 6 above discussed general mistakes to avoid and some heavily tested subjects within larger topics, including authentic acts. Some of the common mistakes to avoid specifically as to authentic acts, and tested frequently, include:

- Incomplete appearances, such as domicile (not residence) and neglecting the statutory requirement of change in marital status (not just marital history) where it's required, including even a status of "no change."
- Capacities and disqualifications, such as that the witnesses not have an interest in the act, or witnesses disqualified by age or other statutory incapacity.
- Forgetting the formal requirements of an authentic act, especially two witnesses—and the necessity that the witnesses and notary watch the party sign.
- Neglecting statutory requirements, such as the full names of all parties, witnesses, and notary placed beneath the signature (the latter easy to forget when so many of the sample forms in the guide, especially in ch. 19 and 29, inexplicably have a signature line drawn but don't add "printed or typed name" under the line, to remind you).
- Forgetting that a certain document must be in authentic form (or thinking one has to that doesn't, like a trust *inter vivos* or act of sale), which is our next chapter.

9

"AA": Acts Required to Be Authentic Acts or in Authentic Form

Every course of study emphasizes how crucial the study guide's pp. 326-27 are. All the acts and instruments that must be in "authentic form" (and not just "authenticated," as discussed below in ch. 11) are spelled out. If you tab or color-edge the book at all, it's probably to make it easy to reach *that* page in a flash. At some point that's unnecessary, because it's the one page (well, two) you come back to so often in your study that you'll have no problem finding it exam day. Anyway, you *will* use it the day of the test.

The magic pages can become even more functional if they're annotated by hand with more page numbers than they already have, so that the list serves as a more complete mini-index to all authentic acts. Lately, the book does include page references, which we've repeated here, plus we've added more in **bold** below you should write onto the bulletpoint list, too.

It's not exactly true that they included *all* authentic acts on these pages. You'll find it helpful to write in the extra situations (or contexts more specific than the magic pages say) that use authentic acts or are in authentic form. They are set out below in **bold**, too, adding page references.

Also on this expanded list we've inserted some situations involving testaments that require the kind of ritual and two witnesses that are characteristic of the authentic act. This reminds you that these contexts, too, have to conform to what might be called authentic form. The study guide used to have them on their list. They took them off in 2021, likely because they *technically* are not the same as authentic acts—in the sense that more is required, it's not enough for a will to have the bare minimum process of authentic form. But since they do *at least* require the ritual and witnesses of an authentic act, it's OK to have them on this reminder list. And we do.

It is also important that, at every place in the book where an act is discussed that must be in authentic form, you mark it in a way that you can't miss, during the exam, the reminder that this event must be done authentically. I don't think highlighting "authentic form" or the like in the text is enough. It's best to use some unique, loud note at each place where authentic form is required, and one such way is explained here:

I've provided this expanded list, with fuller pagination. It's best not to copy it mindlessly, but engage it and follow the cross-references to find the place where that page says "authentic"—then *write **AA** in the margin at each spot*, maybe in your thickest marker or its own color. Every time you get to that act or situation in the book during the exam, you'll be reminded by the bold **AA** that this will need two witnesses and follow all statutory formalities like a full name (p. 339) and names written or printed below the signature (p. 346).

Why is it so crucial to have a list handy of authentic acts and to annotate each place in the guide where they say it's required to be that? Because it's so tested. They are not likely to ask it in the form of "which of the following must be authentic acts?" But there will be someplace (or more) on the exam where they show an example that's missing some essential element of an authentic act, such as witness signatures. It's only "missing" if the act is authentic. Or they'll ask which people have to sign a document (as they do in a sample exam question, p. 733), and you have to name the witnesses and notary as part of the list they give.

Or the exam can have a list of acts in a question and ask which one is invalid if ... [noting an example that does not conform to authentic requirements]. So, the answer is the one that *must* be an authentic act. A good *decoy* answer is one that often *is* in authentic form, but doesn't have to be, such as a document creating a trust *inter vivos* (p. 529 specifies that it could also be accomplished by witness acknowledgment). In these decoy situations, where authentic acts are sufficient but not required, it's **important** that you ***not*** write "AA" there. *Don't highlight the "authentic" in the text*, as it may catch your eye during the exam and trick you into assuming that it *needs* to be authentic. Instead, consider a different note to yourself (because these situations are so testable and counterintuitive); for example, you could use bold initials in the margin and explain it there in smaller print: ***AAAA***: ALLOWS ALTERNATE TO AA (or: acceptable alternative to AA). The study guide includes a list of some such situations at p. 329.

Speaking of counterintuitive, it may help to conceptualize *when* AA is essential—explaining most of the magic pages—in order to develop an intuition that seems second-hand during the exam (still, quickly check the open book to confirm your instinct when actually answering the question). It's an organizing principle. By instinct, ask yourself: what situations in real life *ought to* require the maximum formality and seriousness, and be witnessed in front of a notary by two responsible ("competent") undersigning people?

The answer makes sense if you imagine *two sets of life issues* where you would not *trust* anything less than serious procedure and having witnesses. Two types of things the main signer is trying to accomplish where, cynically, it's awfully tempting to fake an identity or pretend someone else is OK with the result.

One set is situations in which family-shattering changes will result. Giving up children, adopting them, and even allowing people to make parental-type situations are the epitome of fundamental family change. One shouldn't be allowed paternity of your kid without following the letter of the law. If it's not going to be done *in court*, and we allow it to be done privately at all, at least we should make sure you're who you say you are! And add a solemnity that confirms you're really sure you want to give up, say, parenthood of a child that is biologically yours.

9 • ACTS REQUIRED TO BE AUTHENTIC

Even naming someone as a tutor (guardian) is a serious thing and ought to have formalities to make it so.

A second set is situations in which property is immediately and permanently transferred, such as a donation that is totally one-way and not some kind of swap or repayment (contrast *onerous* and *remunerative* donations at pp. 149-51, the difference often tested). We simply cannot assume that someone meant to do such a gratuitous gift if they aren't physically there to sign the instrument making that happen. Imagine if Bob shows up in your notary office with a letter from Jane purporting to give Bob her hunting camp in St. Francisville. Bob is definitely Bob and is willing to sign it. But *of course* he is: he's *getting* the camp. If you could notarize that validly and it effectively transferred the camp just by Bob signing, the camp becomes Bob's without any real proof that this is what *Jane* wanted. And she'd have to hope Bob will give it back to her, because the transfer is immediate and *done*. Good luck with that!

As you can see, we don't allow such transfers on the say-so of the recipient/beneficiary who stands to gain, or even on the written instruction of the giver or seller. Even if the giver's letter is notarized or a proper affidavit. The lack of two witnesses and solemn ritual makes even the giver's notarized letter insufficient to create such a huge property-altering result.

That's true even if property is transferred only at your death: it's a serious thing and fraud is so tempting if it's not clear that the person designating who gets what (and who's cut out) is the actual testator. So even testaments by notary must be made like an authentic form, even if it's not the typical AA and has its own structure and rules (like signature at bottom of each page), as exampled on pp. 512-14 of the study guide and discussed in our next chapter.

Oddly, an olographic (handwritten) will is not made in authentic form, so it's an AAAA. The test-makers will be very clear when they talk about a testament that it's a notarial one—or the document for the scenario is clearly a notary's version, not handwritten. And they are unlikely to ask much if anything about olographic wills (since by definition a notary is not involved), except perhaps to test the will-fail at pp. 637-38 where someone tried to hybridize the notary type with the olographic one—the notarized date did not substitute for the required testator-written one. BTW, in other states it's "holographic," but not actually 3-D.

In short, legal actions that have monumental importance (e.g., declaring you disabled from making choices about your own life) or invoke healthy skepticism (like someone just giving away a property out of love, to the immediate exclusion of the giver and other people who may want it) tend to require that, if they be done just through a notary, they be authentic in every sense of the word.

At any rate, when you study the magic pages and their legendary list of AA-required documents, keep in mind the two sets of situations where it just makes sense that, short of a court order, the result will not happen without the most serious of notarial acts. And the most serious ritual and double-verification we use in Louisiana, outside of court, is the authentic act.

Here's a way to make pp. 326-27 even more magical: make it more complete, and add further cross-reference page numbers in the study guide where the act is detailed. At least, please correct the page cites in the study guide that are wrong!

ACTS REQUIRED TO BE IN AUTHENTIC FORM

Adapted and expanded from C. Alan Jennings et al., *Fundamentals of Louisiana Notarial Law and Practice* (2025 edition), pp. 326-27. Text in **bold** *adds* items or clarifications not found in the study guide's list at those pages, or adds more page numbers of the study guide for cross-referencing (we add the first page of the topic only, not the entire page-range, when it's clear that it continues). You can write the extra entries and page numbers directly into the guide, as between lines in the list. At the very least, hand-correct several **wrong page citations** *in the guide*, shown below in bold italics *["really"]*.

Note required signing order for all authentic acts: parties → witnesses → notary

The following acts or instruments must be *authentic acts* **("AA")** per Civil Code article 1833 in order to be valid (meaning: are absolutely *null* if not AA or in "authentic form"):

- act of surrender (adoption) (Children's Code art. 1122)

- release of claims by alleged father; consent to adoption (Children's Code art. 1196)

- consent of parent to the adoption of child in an intrafamily adoption (Children's Code art. 1244)

- acknowledgment of paternity (C.C. arts. 190.1, 196; R.S. 40:34.5.2) (pp. 599, **184**), **including 3-party form, 601, 183**

- **revocation of acknowledgment of paternity before 60 days, 600**

- adult adoption (C.C. art. 213) (pp. 186 *[really, it's 185]*, 602)

- **provisional custody by mandate: effectively AA when using statutory forms (of R.S. 9:954, 962), 630**

- designation of tutor ("tutorship by will") other than in a testament **(i.e., if done inter vivos it's AA)** (C.C. art. 257) (see pp. 190, 615)

- limited emancipation by authentic act (C.C. art. 368) (see pp. 192, 616)

- modification or termination of limited emancipation by authentic act (C.C. art. 371) (see pp. 193, 617)

- declaration of dispensation from collation when made by separate later act (C.C. art. 1232) (see *Caveat Notarius* below, **327**)

- proof of conditions of partnership to exempt from collation (C.C. art. 1247) (see *When writing is required*, p. 583)

- gratuitous transfer of separate property to the community (C.C. art. 2343.1) (see pp. 147 *[really, it's 134]*, 206) **(even for movables)**

- donations inter vivos of immovables and incorporeal things (and corporeal movables when not effected by actual delivery, or when the donation must be in writing) (C.C. arts. 1541) (see pp. 145-48) ... **But not remunerative nor onerous donations (the latter just in writing, if immovable), unless *donation in disguise* so not truly remunerative or onerous, 149-51**

- **donative transfer of a motor vehicle *title* is included in the above (must be AA to have OMV accept it, unless new-car dealer), but transfer of actual ownership may be done by manual gift, 148, 152, 434**

- confirmation **after-the-fact** of donations by the donor during his lifetime that were required to be by authentic act but which are null for lack of proper form (C.C. art. 1842, 1845) (see p. 642 *[really, it's 146]*; also *Confirmation of donation*, p. 642)

- **notarial testaments (C.C. arts. 1577-1580.1) are like their own type of AA, 470**

- **revocation of entire testaments(s) by testator in an AA (C.C. arts. 1607) ... Will can also be revoked by a new will, either notarial or olographic, and by other means, 483**

- **notarial codicils are like notarial wills, using form like AA, 509**

- act of mortgage or privilege **(including vendor's lien in credit sale)** on immovable property importing *confession of judgment* in order to proceed by *executory process* (C.C.P. arts. 2631, 2635) (see p. 391)

- declaration of immobilization of a mobile home when not contained in a validly executed and acknowledged sale, mortgage, or sale with mortgage (R.S. 9: 1149.4) (see p. 387; **see generally 87, 89**)

- beneficiary's *refusal* of interest in an *inter vivos* trust (R.S. 9:1985) (see p. 532 *[really, it's 542]*)

- **similarly, renunciation by heir or legatee *in favor of another* acts like acceptance then donation, so must be AA, 462; but general renunciation need only be in writing, 461**

- grant of real right in immovable property created for educational, charitable, or historic purposes (R.S. 9:1252)

- act to establish disability of principal in conditional procuration (R.S. 9: 3890) (see p. 251); **more on POA below**

- act of sale of titled movable sold by holder of privilege (R.S. 9:4502)

- act to cancel mortgage or privilege secured by paraphed obligation (R.S. 9:5170) (see p. 300), **but 2 non-AA supporting docs may be used instead of an act, 300 ("or")**

- unincorporated association statement of authority (R.S. 12:505) (see pp. 395, **598**)

- **consent by LLCs (of up to 5 members), for representative to appear for it before state entities, 598**

- act of correction by notary **(a/k/a affidavit of correction)** (R.S. 35: 2.1) (see pp. 603); **act of correction by parties, <u>if</u> underlying act was AA, 605, ... but affidavit of correction for *vehicle* title need not be AA, 439**

- **affidavit of distinction, if using the optional statutory form, is effectively AA (at least, requires 2 Ws), 606**

- power of attorney authorizing any act **that itself is** required to be in authentic form (C.C. art. 2993) (see p. 252): **POA must be AA, to be effective, *if* what it's authorizing (like donation) requires AA**

- **But 4 things cannot be done by POA: will, affidavit, marriage, adult adoption** [a list we also note in our ch. 15, below]

Similar to this list, the study guide has a less-magical and shorter list of acts that are only valid if they are authentic acts *or* acknowledged acts. We discuss at the beginning of this chapter how important it is not to think of this list as acts requiring authentic form (instead, they are "AAAA"). Here, I'll just add that two of the cross-references on p. 329 are incorrect and need to be corrected in your guide, since they take you to the wrong page (like those for AA noted above). These are the ones for matrimonial agreement, where the guide cites p. 326 but means <u>208</u>; and for reservation of fruits, which cites p. 200 but means <u>201</u>.

10

Notarial Testaments and Successions

The "testament," a/k/a "will," is simply a donation made upon death (*mortis causa*). Like donations made while still living (*inter vivos*), it must be done in an authentic form. At least, when done with a notary—when not "olographic."

The same concept of an authentic act effectively applies to the *notarial testament*, with some additional language and requirements. So the outline structure given earlier for other such acts generally applies to wills, too—with minor variations in the kind of appearance clause used (for example, it sets out residential address instead of domicile), and a major difference in the attestation clause's exact language you are expected to use for a notarial testament.

But it's different enough overall—and an excellent, annotated example is in the study guide at pp. 512-14—that, to answer questions, you can use the book's own exemplar and ch. 24 instead of your notes about similarly authentic acts.

Still, keep in mind the related *idea*, the shared sense that they are all events which the notary emcees and doesn't just attest to. Much the same warnings apply: if you remember it's an action and not just a paper, it makes sense to have the witnesses see the testator sign it, and in an exact order (pp. 636-37); it makes sense that special rules apply for testators who are impaired in some way (pp. 472-76); and it makes sense that witnesses to a testament be more "competent" and less conflicted (pp. 351-53) than they have to be in other settings.

All such acts use magic words at very specific places in the document (just as the jurat is the magic for an affidavit). But the words change for this different context: donating property upon death. Its own special catchphrases, such as the attestation clause dictated by statute, are routinely tested.

To the extent it is not clear from the book's annotated example, and an incomplete, textual components list on p. 470, here is the structure of the typical testament (to write into the book, e.g., at p. 511):

- venue
- title
- appearance
- dispositive portion
- testator signature after that (+ bottom all other pages)
- date (can be elsewhere, but often is near testator signature)

- attestation clause
- 2 witnesses' signatures (+ names under)
- notary's signature (+ name and notary # printed under, or stamped)

Having an author-approved example of a valid will makes it easier if they do ask a question that tests your understanding of the rules and terms. Most likely the question would draw on some clarification in the sample's footnote annotations, such as the difference between a *universal* legacy and a *particular* one. They certainly may test your remembering that each page before the signature page also has the testator's signature at the bottom. So, go ahead and draw a big star next to the name-lines shown on these pages.

But since the good example is there and easy to locate, it's more likely they will give you an *imperfect* example as a partial document near the scenario, and make you explain (in multiple choice) why it's invalid, or figure out ways to make it valid. Some features of the will they provide may look menacing, such as that the notary is named as an executor or trustee as well, leading you to look elsewhere in the chapter to be sure that's allowed (it's OK, see p. 481; notary can't be *legatee*).

Note that a sample testament, unlike the one they provide at the end of the chapter, may also be written in the third person, sounding more like an affidavit than the sample in the guide does (which says "I" for the testator). By itself that's not a problem as long as the core, dispositive portion is written in the first person. The notary is just introducing the testator. An example of a valid will that does have some third-person POV to it is shown below in ch. 18, just so you wouldn't be thrown off too much by the change in perspective from the exemplar in the guide. The will isn't an affidavit, and not written using a jurat, but it can be *introduced* in the third person (from the notary's POV) the way other acts are.

Ultimately, it's a statement of the testator's intent, not the notary's or anyone else's. It is a *singular* event, not only in the sense of "important," but also two people can't join to make one testament (p. 468). That's unlike many acts, and even some affidavits like the small succession one of ch. 27, which contemplates a group verification of assets and agreement—multiple signers.

The examiners often combine a will situation with other substantive issues that make you look beyond ch. 24 for an answer to the specific question asked. They often create a trust in the will (ch. 25), or ask questions about the succession that follows, or test on the usufruct as a byproduct of the will (or of intestate inheritance). Sometimes a question seemingly about a testament may be less about the will as such; instead it is used as a steppingstone to test understanding of community property ownership and transfer, donations, family relations such as emancipation or tutorship, or trust law.

As for successions, they often test the small succession procedure (often called now "succession by affidavit," since there are some instances where even large estates worth more than $125,000 can take advantage of it). They use successions to test your understanding of usufruct and community property, for example that the estate of the deceased technically doesn't include the surviving spouse's share of the community. With such scenarios they often make you do math, believe it or not, for instance to determine whether the remaining estate qualifies as a small succession (see our ch. 17 below).

Successions without a valid will are "intestate"—and they often test the term for that, as well as "heirs" (intestate donees) versus "legatees" (receive by testacy, i.e., in a will). No notary is involved in intestate succession (unless one wrote an invalid will that fails, so it's *the same as* "intestate"—a plausible situation to get tested). So you may think they wouldn't ask about it. But the rules of succession are the kind of general Louisiana property law they expect you to learn well, or at least index well and be able to answer the day of the exam. Particularly because intestate inheritance affects several aspects of testate succession.

One instance when the testate/intestate rules formally overlap, and become testable, is when the percentage of an estate must be left to a child through forced heirship regardless of the testator's intent. The percentage—more math—may be a function of the number of forced heirs and the default they would get if the decedent had no will (explained below, pp. 113-15). So, you have to know intestate succession, which itself doesn't have forced heirship, even in a testate succession where forced legacies are potentially involved.

Finally, they often test other rules of forced heirship. Two huge subjects: (1) a forced heir can be 24+ if they are disabled at the time of decedent's passing, including situations like debilitating bipolarism more subtle than a wheelchair (p. 485), and (2) the grounds for disinheriting a forced heir are limited and statutory (p. 495); for exam purposes, they're non-negotiable and you can't go off the list to name one that doesn't fit the accepted situations allowing disinherison. If it's not literally on the list, the answer is: the legacy is forced.

The subject of testaments, successions, and community property law is pervasive and difficult, but the study guide never quite presents the big picture. The details are there, and can be indexed by subtopic, yet most students also need a way to wrap their heads around the whole. Our ch. 17 attempts to visualize the concept for you. Now's the time to turn to the final "Notarial A," but if you have difficulty with wills and related subjects, that chapter on wills and community property may be helpful.

11

Acknowledged Acts

The full name is "acts under private signature duly acknowledged," and that indicates the actual process used: private acts (just signed writings) turned into something more by coming to a notary. But it's fine to call them *acknowledged acts*. They may also be called "authenticated acts," though that's too close to "authentic acts" to keep straight, so it's best not to use the term. The latter term does capture the notion that such instruments are self-proving in court—they are technically "authenticated" for purposes of admission into evidence without having to use a witness at trial to verify they're real.

That self-proving quality of acknowledged acts is shared with the full-blown authentic act. Both self-prove (study guide pp. 164, 331), which is important in how the document is used at law. But for notary exam purposes, it's likely that the examiners focus more on the main difference between the two acts: where a situation requires an authentic act (see above, ch. 9).

The authentic act is perhaps far more often tested on the notary exam because it comes up in more notarial contexts than do acknowledged ones. Still, a question on acknowledged acts is predictable because it forces you to sort through two wholly different versions of such acts, as discussed in the study guide at pp. 330-31 and explained on our next page.

So, the two most likely key points to be tested: (1) these two different options for acknowledging a private act, easily confused, and (2) the relatively few situations in which an acknowledged act works as a fair substitute for the authentic act, or even is required for a document to be valid (not just self-proving) if it's not truly authentic.

The best example of number 2 is an instrument creating a trust *inter vivos* (p. 529). I suggested in ch. 9 that when you see such examples in the study guide, boldly mark AAAA in the margin to remind you on test day that it's *not* on the magic list of acts requiring authentic form (pp. 326-27). In most such AAAA situations, the law requires *either* an authentic act *or* an acknowledged one.

The study guide clarifies that, to get the self-proving benefit of an acknowledged act, all you need is a private act and an acknowledgment. In such cases there is that courtroom efficiency of proof, but the legal action is still valid as a private act when the parties signed it, no notary in sight. But there are a number of situations (which you can designate by AAAA) where the act is not effective until it is properly acknowledged. It's not just about proving the parties sign it: it's also a requirement for the act to activate. The *timing* of effectiveness is not the private signing but the later acknowledgment. A list of such situations, notably the trust one above and a matrimonial agreement, is on p. 329. It's not quite the magic list of AA-required acts, but it's close—a "hybrid," the textbook says (p. 328). Certainly in all such situations an AA would be enough, too.

A harder question, because it is not just a matter of scavengering the answer from that list or the margin of your guide, would test your understanding of my number 1 above: the two different *ways*, using two different statutory bases, a notary can authenticate a private act signed outside the presence of the notary. Even though the answer may be figured out by applying pp. 330-31, that snippet is confusing, so a big picture and example may make it clearer.

To step back a bit: both situations involve something signed outside the notary's presence (earlier in time) and both involve two witnesses; the key difference is *when* those witnesses get involved. Almost by definition, both contexts fail to have both parties to the transaction before the notary, since then it could easily be done by *authentic act* simply by having it witnessed there. So the context for an acknowledged act usually is one where the notary has only *one* of the two parties in their office. The two contexts both fill a need to have the document be more than just signed even if it is less than authentic. They both scratch an itch for something to be self-proving even if it amounts to "authentic-light."

Picture two parties in an IHOP who agree to a deal, scrawl out the terms on a paper, and both sign it. What if they want it to be more than just a private act, to be something that holds up in court without having to haul the parties there to introduce the contract into evidence? (Or it's on that list where it can *only* be valid once it gets acknowledged, if not AA.) But one party can't make it to your office?

The law gives them two great options short of the authentic act, both requiring a notary and two witnesses. They differ mainly in *when* the witnesses do their job. (Btw, if the problem is just that they both can't show up together, they could still do it as an authentic act by each executing it separately before different notaries—or the same notary at different times—just as many documents are executed separately but combine to be treated as one, pp. 634-36. We'll ignore this 'counterparts' shortcut here, since that result is simply 'authentic' if done right.)

If two people watching in IHOP served as witnesses, that's half the battle. But without witnesses *then and there*, you'll need two at the notary's office. Either option of authenticating a private act needs two witnesses *at some point*. The two methods, with two different statutory sources, are:

Acknowledgment by party *(C.C. art. 1836)*

After an act under private signature was made, one party goes to the notary and acknowledges it, recognizing the prior signature as his or her own in front of two [new] witnesses. This way doesn't necessarily have to be witnessed when it was originally signed.

11 ▪ ACKNOWLEDGED ACTS

So the IHOP-deal made with no witnesses at the scene can still be authenticated, after the fact, by having either party confirm it in front of the notary and two witnesses—as long as the notary collects those signatures in the proper order as with an authentic act (party, witnesses, then notary) and as long as the requirements of Title 35 are met (e.g., witnesses' names below the signatures). The procedure to do this is in the form of an acknowledgment of an existing document.

Acknowledgment by affidavit of prior witness, grantor, or vendor (R.S. 13:3720)

After an act under private signature was made, and properly witnessed *at the time* with two witnesses, the instrument can be acknowledged by an affidavit (before a notary) made either: (1) by the vendor or grantor swearing he did sign it in front of the witnesses, or, most usefully, (2) by one or both of the [original] witnesses setting forth that the instrument had been executed before them. In the latter version, a party essentially drags a witness to the notary (or the witness goes alone) and makes the instrument more official than it would otherwise be. A witness acknowledgment of this kind (#2) is shown below at p. 119.

At the IHOP, where witnesses saw the parties sign the napkin, one (or both, but why bother?) can go with a party and execute the affidavit (and actually could go without a party). Or the party—if it's the one giving away the interest—can go without either of the prior witnesses but swear to the witnessed paper-signing before. Why the one *giving* the interest? We're more skeptical of the *recipient* of property or an interest; the one who's giving it away is less likely to be doing it fraudulently. In our IHOP example, if it's a valid and mutual exchange, either party could be considered a grantor or vendor. If they test this option, my guess is they would make it clearly a vendor (seller), or make it clearly the opposite party (buyer) so this option is not available—but then remember that party could use the other method, requiring two *new* witnesses at the notary.

They may also test this option by relating it to a more general rule about affidavits: these are personal to the affiant, and cannot be delegated to an agent or mandatary. The procedure to do this option is in the form of an affidavit about a previous event—the signing—and an existing document. It would be a wrong answer to have someone else claim to be acting on behalf of the party, even with all the paperwork to show they have that mandate (a power of attorney to act for the party), since this option is an affidavit.

Similarly, an affidavit not made before a notary cannot be made valid by witness acknowledgment (p. 334).

A third form? Car title transfers (+ a note on vehicle donations)

Although it's not presented in ch. 19 on acknowledgments, in reality there's another situation where a witness matters after-the-fact much like the "affidavit of prior witness" version just above. That's when a vehicle buyer and seller want to transfer title but they aren't both going to the notary, a situation found in ch. 23 of the study guide.

The usual way would be for buyer and seller to show up to the notary and sign ("endorse") the certificate of title (often also with a bill of sale, p. 434, though it's usually not required). Even just the *seller* signing in front of a notary will do (p. 427). But otherwise, the back of the certificate allows the transfer—though it was not first signed before a notary—by having it signed by the seller, as witnessed by two witnesses who also sign at the time (in the left column). Then one of the witnesses goes to the notary and acknowledges the prior signing, here in the longer text below the columns. The notary verifies the witness's signing there. A textual version of this process is also laid out on pp. 427-28.

This is a useful process, much like the R.S. 13:3720 one for various documents, in situations where it's anticipated that one party (usually, seller) is finished with the transaction by signing at someone's home or work, but no notary handy. The OMV still regards the certificate and vehicle as transferred—after it's witnessed at the notary's office and the title's acknowledgment block is signed. The certificate of title actually builds the whole witness acknowledgment into its back (p. 431: "a witness to the signature(s) of seller(s)").

A sample bill of sale is provided below, in our ch. 18. But an act of donation would be used to transfer a car, boat, trailer, etc. without compensation. This usually needs to be an authentic act, and with written acceptance by the donee, for OMV to issue a new certificate of title—as the study guide emphasizes in several spots, e.g., p. 434, and thus is very possibly tested.

By the way, and unrelated to using witnesses to fill the gap, the absent party in a car deal could also empower someone to go to the notary for him or her, by using a power of attorney. Often that's done, for example, when there are two owners listed on the front page, but one is going to take the lead in the sales process.

12

Index and Additional Definitions

The following expanded, annotated index is meant to be hand-copied right into the existing glossary (though another method is mentioned below, next page). Because many questions can only be answered by looking in two or more places in the book (and not all information is found at the obvious site for that subject), finding all mentions of a topic is essential. Copying it for exam day will make a few extra questions, and probably even more than a few, answerable under the pressure and time limits they impose. Because even a few extra points here or there is crucial, having access to all places a subject is mentioned may well spell the difference between pass and fail.

Your own hand-inserted index need not be as duplicative or exhaustive as the below. It just needs to lead you to the right parts of the book during the exam, and deal with the fact that the relevant information is often spread across two or more places in the book. Still, my goal is to make it usable during the time-limited and nerve-wracking test. To that end, I don't follow the norms of indexing—such as efficiency of having only one entry for an idea—because users need to find the page references fast, in the first place they look (e.g., including both "pet trust" and "animal trust"; or both "surviving spouse" and "spouse, surviving"). So, repeating info fully in two or more entries will save time.

Likewise, I don't tend to cross-reference with words only (like "will—see testament"), instead writing the same page numbers in both places There's also limited room in the glossary, so I use some abbreviations (you'll likely use more, or shorter ones), and I state things very briefly—just enough to point you to the guide's discussion. I break three other norms of indexing, though you don't have to, as you write it into the guide.

First, it's not perfect alphabetical order. Items have to be inserted where there happens to be space between glossary words. The open space doesn't occur in perfect order. I'm not worried you'll miss spying an entry that's a few words away from where it should be; I *am* worried you won't fit it all in if you ignore open space just to stay in line. I try to keep order, sure, but you'll see the list below is often fitted to where there's room to write.

Second, true indexes name the range of pages for a topic (like "pp. 61-62"), but I usually list the *first page only*. It's enough to get you to where the topic starts, and you'll readily see the conversation continues to the next page. Only where the range of pages is more than a few pages, or you might miss the globality of the topic, do I use ranges. There's a whole section on predial servitudes, so I cover the whole, for instance.

Third, I don't always list the page numbers in ascending order. Where there's a page you clearly should go to first, I put it first ("348, 40, 600"). I don't want to skip any page that mentions the topic, but often there's a *key* place to look and some related pages. They do test your ability in one question to put together info from two places in the book, so all listed pages are potentially useful. But some are more on-point or thorough than others. This artifice is truly optional since it may confuse some who'd prefer to re-right the page order; just do so as you copy it. But really you want *prioritization* and not just "any mentions." I'm hoping the first place you look works. Or in reviewing, note the first page you should read. (You could also right the order but underline the most important number.)

Note that I put in **bold**, below, any terms that are *already in the glossary*. This isn't meant to *emphasize* them, just to indicate it's already there and you only need to insert numbers or an added thought (not in bold). I use many subentries (sorted by semi-colons, or new lines with hyphens) where thoughts are broken down. Parsing concepts is a valuable indexing norm that helps on exam day.

This index is meant to be handwritten into the book's glossary, but it's best not to make it only a mindless copying task. Sure, the first round of that can be done in front of the TV or while watching a child's swim practice. At some point you need to *engage* the index and follow the main points to their specific page, especially the first page mentioned that is most instructive. You should see this index as a dialog and aid to the studying process, not just as a list to copy. This is like how I noted earlier (ch. 9) that just adding page numbers to the magic-AA-page is not as effective as also using it to go write "AA" boldly by the source text. Here, too, it's best to use the index to go find the main point assigned and to be familiar with what's around it. It's about better studying, not just open-book testing. Yet even copying it mechanically may be decisive for the exam.

I advise using the *glossary* as the basis, to save the blank pages at the back for other uses. The glossary's already there and in ABC order, and has many entries that need page cites (plus some just defined but never found in the book itself). It just seemed more efficient to me to use the glossary. But several past users say they created an independent index in the blank pages, and don't have to fit it in the smaller glossary open space. If you do that, be sure to write all the bolded words (already in the glossary) and indicate some way they are defined in the glossary (asterisk, the letter G, underlining—anything obvious on exam day). That way you won't be checking the glossary too, to see it's there as well. But I do advise using the glossary to index, if only because the definitions will be right there too, and you won't have to look in two places to see its meaning.

This chapter is an important part of our book. A reader *could* copy and share it. We'd appreciate it if you'd respect the copyright of this work and *not* do that. We priced the book low (with very cheap ebooks) so that anyone who wanted any part of it could buy it. Hopefully users will share their *awareness* of this index with others—and share their views, pro or con, about it and the tips in this book—but not copy it. (And I need to justify the effort to rewrite this book each year, only possible if it's not given away.) Thanks for considering that reality.

12 • INDEX AND ADDITIONAL DEFINITIONS

INDEX AND ADDITIONAL EXPLANATIONS

Notes:
- **bold** = already a glossary entry; bold *isn't* used here to mean emphasis
- some glossary terms, bold, don't have a page number if the entry suffices
- -- means a subentry; this is also done on one line divided by semi-colons
- page number listed is often the first page of discussion; few page *ranges*
- alphabetical order is deviated from when there's more space, nearby, to insert new entry into existing glossary
- page numbers may not be in ascending order; first entry is most useful
- some abbreviations or short statements are used here; you can use more

abstract (relates to ch. 22)

acceleration clause 389

acceptance of donation 134, 385; of manual gift, 148

accessory contract 168

accessory obligation (mortg=access'y; promissory note=primary), 288

accessory thing 95 (e.g. car key)

accession 91-95
  -- of movables 95

accretion:
  1. improvement to prop 92
  2. successions: increase to heir/legatee 461, 478, 458
  3. trust: increase to beneficiary 541

acknowledged act 328-33

acknowledgment 330, 163
  -- forms of ackn 332, 359, 694
  -- foreign 695

acknowledgment of paternity 182-84, 599-602
  -- revoking it, also AA 600
  -- 3-party ackn 183, 601

acquets and gains 199

acquisition of sep prop, decl of, 205

acquisitive prescription 96, 121

acquittance 380

act under private signature 328, 163

Act of Congress 626

act of correction (='affid of corr'): by notary, 603, 661 (is AA); by parties, 604 (AA if orig. act was)
  -- for car title 439 (='affid of corr'), *not* AA
  -- not used for wills 510 (must be in testamentary form)

act of deposit 355

act of sale, immovs 368, 335; titled movs ('bill of sale') 434

administrator 490

adult adoption 185; form: 602 (AA)

advanced directive 488 ('living will'); witness not relative: 351

affiant 333, 338, 343

affidavit 333, 343-45; form: 361
  -- oath 365-67; alternatives to swear, 344, 345; oath of office, 365, 67

affidavit of correction; *see* act of correction

affidavit of distinction 605
    (also called affidavit of identifi-

cation or identity), 607, 290
-- for car: 'one & the same person,' 440

affid of 'death and heirship' 510, 603

affid of heirship 437 (get car before success'n)

age of testator 465; +other donors 130
-- of witness, 351; but W to *will* is 16+: 353, 481

agent ch 15; *see* mandatary & POA

agreement ch 11; *see* contract

agreement to sell or buy ch 13

aleatory contract 168

alien: as notary 64; as heir 456, 481

alienate ch 13, 21

aliquot part 404

alluvion 92

alternatives for appearances 634-36; alternative to 'swear' 344, 345

ancillary succession 565

antichresis (now superseded) 274

'ancient document' 40 (if recorded >10 yrs: presume signed by signer)

animals: trusts 525-27 (=pet trust); if it's immovable 87

antenuptial agreement 617, 208, 329 (bef marry *or* move to LA <1 yr)

Apostilles 43

appearance clause, 338-43; forms: 357-59
-- diff parties at diff times (or >1 notary) 362, 636, 163
-- spouses 340, 356, 663
-- affidavits require too 335

appearer 339 (role or capacity)

appointment of notary 63, 669

appraisal ch 26

articles of incorporation 586, 31; must be English 586; contrast partnrship 579

articles of organization 593 (for LLC: also in Engl.)

appurtenances (relates to ch 8)

ascendant (direct line up, not collaterals), 453, 187

'as is' clause 648, 319

assignment 154, 158, 241, 354, 427, 597

assumption of obligation 158

assumption deed (relates to ch 21)

attachments, form for 362
-- very limited for wills 509

attest: compare to swear 344, 345

attorney in fact ch 15; *see* mandatary

attorney fees, in mortg, 390; in promissory note, 392

Attorney General: opinions not law 34
-- AG or DA files 'show cause' rule against notary 665

authentic act 321-27, 162-64; history of 8-9; formalities crucial 638-42; acts required to be 326-27

base line 402

beneficiary 536; defn., 517-18; 'institutional,' 519; class trust 519

bequest ch 24; defn.='legacy,' 476; 'bequeath' shows donative intent, 507

biological parents/surrogacy 182, 455

bill of sale 434, 215

birth certif 613 (no 'true copy')

blanks in forms/contracts 650

blind testator 473; blind & deaf 475;

12 • INDEX AND ADDITIONAL DEFINITIONS

blind W 353, 481 (+ W if T blind)

bond ch 16; of notaries, 65-67, 667

bond, personal surety 66

bond-for-deed contract 373 (not yet a sale), homestead exemption 375

boundary line 424, 409

bribery 47

Building Contractor's Lien 608, 153

building restrictions 127

business: authenticate docs for (or family), 651

business entities, ch 28

by root 457 (=per stirpes)

cancellation of a mortgage 299-305 (≠ partial release)

capacity 130, 320, 339 (incl juridical person & represnt'ves)

-- contracts 168; legal vs. contractual 130, 168

-- to donate or accept 130, 465, 451, 481

-- to make a will 465, 503, 130; duress 505, 170; trust 529

-- of witness generally 351; but for will 481, 353 (age 16+)

-- notary as executor is OK, 351, 481

car/vehicle: sale or transfer title, ch 23

-- donation of 434, 644, 148

-- fix title error by affid of correction 439

-- get car before succession 437; form: 436

cash sale 368 (AA not req'd)

cash deed 368

cause, required for contract 171

certif of authority (LLC) 395

certif of custodian private docs 614

certified copy, varieties: 611-14, 162; but not birth certif 613

chattel ... chattel mortg, 308, 59

change of name 185, 197

charitable trust 519

charter 586 (=articles of incorp)

Civil Code 15, 29; origins 16

civil fruits 92

citizen as heir, 456; as legatee, 481; as notary 64 (none has to be)

class trust 519

code ch 5

codicil 509

coercion of testator 505, 170

collateral 284 (security for loan)

collateral mortgage 307-13

collaterals 453 (e.g. siblings)

collation 326-27, 583; dispense with in partnrship contract, is AA 327, 583

commission of notary: issued, 67; keep 68; suspend 52-54, 665

common law, compared, 14, 249

common things 83

community property 200-04, 458; not a juridical person 202

competency of witness; *see* capacity

component parts of tracts of land 88, 86

-- who owns? 94

concurrence 202; renunciation of, 203

conditional obligation 155

conditional procuration 251

confession of judgment 391, 389 (allows executory process) confirmation of donation 146, 642, 174-76

confusion 126 (really, whole book?)

conflict of interest: wills, 504
-- notarize for business/family 651
-- notary in bank/employee 56, 651; as agent 55

Congress, Act of: prove notary's status 626

conjoint legacy 477; accretion 478-79

consideration
-- vs. cause 171, 647
-- mistake to say in contract 648

consumables 103

constructive trust 527

contract: 163; types of, 167-68
-- blank spaces in, 650

contractual regime 207 (all sep prop)

conventional mortgage 288, 298

conveyance records 59, 353-56

copies of many acts 611-14, 162

corporation 586-92
-- corp resolution 394
-- form to appear 359
-- attaching corp doc to act, 363

corporeals 85, 88

corpus (trust principal or 'res'), 517

counterparts, sign by 636, 163

counter letter 396

correction, affid of (act of), 603, 661
-- by notary 603 (clerical err.; is AA)
-- by party 604 (AA if orig. act was)
-- for car/vehicle title 439 (not AA)

covenant marriage 197

courts, ch 4; appellate cts 33

credit deed

credit sale 369

cum onere 294; clause 386

custodial trust 520

custodian of private docs (discovery) 614

custodian: nonlegal custd'n affid 618 (med or educ consent)

curator / curatrix 194

corrupt influenc'g 47, 49 (like bribery)

date on will 507, 471; failure of olographic 637, 468

dation en paiement 151, 380

deaf testator 475; deaf W 353, 482

declaration of life-sustaining procedures 351

declaration of acquis of sep prop 205

decedent 446; if goes missing 454; dead body 449, 500

de facto doctrine 69

degree 456-58 (re heirs), 408 (on map)

de jure 70

dereliction 92 (like alluvion)

derogation, acts in 319; such contract is null 165, 174

designate tutor 615, 188

destination: of owner 120; immovable by, 87

detrimental reliance 172

descendants 453 (direct lineage down)

disability, act establishing 251 (after cond'l procurat'n; is AA)

disclaimers 324, 654 ('notary not read')

12 • INDEX AND ADDITIONAL DEFINITIONS

disclosures at closing 397

dishonor 623 (protest re check)

discovery 614

discussion of assets 580

disguised donation 147, 645, 172, 381

disinherison 494-97; method must meet testamentary form 486

dissolution of donation 143

distinction, affid of 605, 290

disposable portion 484, 138

divorce 454; legatee or executor 490, 510; effect on trust 531

documents lost/stolen/destroyed 161

dollar: '$1 & consideration' 646

domicile 339, 180 (≠ residence, 339, 571)

  -- decl intent to change 614, 181

donation inter vivos, ch 10; form & content 383-86, 145

  -- AA req'd, 146; but 4 exceptns 148

  -- d in disguise 147, 645, 172; dation as d in disg 151, 381; must accept 148

  -- d of titled movable 434, 644, 148

  -- d is null, 137-42; cure for (confirm imperfect d) 146, 642, 174-76

  -- d of future prop is null 141, 384

  -- d of naked ownership? 133

  -- prohibited d's (incl all prop) 137

  -- ways to accept d of immov 135, 381; manual gift of mov 136, 148

  -- *who* can accept d, 134

  -- successors can't accept 134, 384-85 (must do bef donor or donee dies)

  -- reserve a usufr? 133

  -- forced portion in a d, 484, 138

  -- trust, d prop to, 546

donation mortis causa (will): 129 & esp. ch 24

donee: *who* can accept 134 (bef either dies)

  -- acceptance in writing by 135

  -- any age may receive (but not accept) 130; unborn child 130, 481

donor: capacity to donate 130; if by will, 465

drawee (receives order of payment)

drawer (writes the check) 624

dual commission 67 (pre-2005 notary)

due-on-sale clause, 375, 389

  -- triggered by bond-for-deed?, 372 (or lease)

durable power of attorney 260

duress of testator 505, 170; of party to AA 162

earnest money

easement 101 (com law predial serv)

electronic signatures 350

emancipation 192, 616

embryo, as heir 455; as legatee or donee 481

enclosed estate 116-17

encumber; encumbrance ch 17-18; accept d by, 135

endorsement for a note: 393; for a car title: 427

English: req'd in art's of incorp 586, 656; & in LLC art's of organizatn 593

  -- *not* always req'd in partnrship contract 579

  -- corp *name* just uses Eng *letters* 588

  -- not needed for will 506, 655, 471

  -- proficiency, for notary, 64

escrow 10, 374

escheat 464

estate 447, 476; can't donate i.v. entire estate 137; but OK in will 465
-- not a juridical pers. 448
-- 'estate' [land] as in predial servitude 113

et seq.

exchange 379

executor 490; appearance clause 358
-- can be notary or legatee 351, 481
-- appointed bef divorce 490, 510

executory process (foreclosure), 390
-- certified copy for 612

executrix 490

express: trust 516; terms in POA 253; donative intent 131, 506; accept d 135

extinction of mortg, 297

fair market value 100, 226, 381, 439; motor veh. 442

false swearing 333

family: authenticating docs for 651

fee simple title: transfer by sale 368

fetus: in will or donation 481, 130
-- natural vs. juridical pers. 179, 455
-- unborn=natr'l pers. 179; not implanted=juridical 180
-- capacity to receive d, 130

fiduciary 463, 518, 592

filiation 182

financed lease 246, 248

financing statement 283

first refusal, right of 387

forced heir 484-86
-- disinheriting 494-97; form 494

-- grandkids, if child dies 485
-- irrelevant if intestate 486

forced portion (=legitime) 484
-- in a trust 547, 486
-- in a d 138, 484

foreign language: acts in, 655
-- wills in, 506
-- art's of incorp or organizatn (no): 586, 593; partnrship contract (can be OK): 579
-- corp name 588 (OK if Eng letters)

foreign trust (not La.) 527, 518

fortuitous event 177

four corners doctrine 345

fruits defined 92; usufruct over 104
-- reservation of fr of sep prop 201

full name 339, 469, 664 (but *signature* can be less 347, 469)

general mortgage 288, 290

general jurisdiction ct (vs. limited) 24

general legacy 467, 476-78, 513 n.10

giving in payment 151, 380 (=dation; e.g. voluntary foreclosure)

good faith 97

gross value 565

guardian 188-91 (as tutor), 194, 615

habitation 110, 155

half-siblings 459

hand note: an IOU, receipt, or prom. note, 308-11

health care POA (med mandate) 254

heir 447, 454 (intestate successor); natural heir 489; forced heir 484, 494

heirship, affid of 437 (to get car)

hereditaments 627

12 • INDEX AND ADDITIONAL DEFINITIONS

heritable 154, 158; servitudes differ on 106, 111, 112

homestead exemption: if bond-for-deed 375; waiver of, in mortgage 390

hypothecate (relates to ch 17)

identity, affid of (=of distinction) 605, 607, 290

illegitimate children 189

immobilization (and de-immobilization) 89
  -- act re mobile home is AA, if separate doc 327, 387
  -- immovable by declaration 87, 89
  -- and leases 247
  -- in act of sale 387

improvements, who owns, 94

immovable 86-90, 93-95
  -- transfer 38 & esp. ch 21
  -- by declaration, destination (incl. animals), & nature 87

imperative laws 319; donation 139

in globo

in rem mortgage 307

in terrorem (no-contest) clause 493, 487

in toto

incorporeal (or non-corporeal) 86, 88; donation of, 148

incorporat'g other docs into acts 362; but into will 509

independ. admin., 491 (don't assume T wants 491, 514 n.17)

informal ackn of paternity 184

infra

indivision 91, 97 [*see* partition]

ingratitude 142, 144

injuring public records 50

inter vivos: donation 129; trust 528

intent: to change domicile 614, 181; donative intent 131, 506, 148

interdict 193

interdiction 193 (notary can't)

interpretation, rules of 165-67

interpretive

interrogatories, verify 633

intestate: succession 453-64

inventory ch 26

investment property 148, 136; investments/IRA/bank acct. not in estate?, 448

joint legacy ('conjoint'), 477, 478-79

judge, district court, 25; suspend notary for cause 23, 52
  -- rule to show cause filed by DA or AG in distr ct, 665

judgment 321 (drafting not allowed); foreign 291

judgment creditor 290

judgment debtor 290

judicial mortgage 290-92, 288

jurat 616; example in affid 361; alternative forms 344

juridical person 180; embryo as, 455, 180
  -- community is *not* JP 202
  -- La. trust not JP 517, nor estate 448
  -- JP as trustee?, 533
  -- as usufructuary 106 (ends ≤ 30 yrs)

just title 96

L.L.C. 592; appearance clause 359

L.L.P. 582

laborer's privilege or lien 608 (=Private Works Act Lien)

landlord (=lessor) ch 14

lapsed legacy 492 (conditional bequest)

lease ch 14

-- reconducted lease 245

-- taking ownership subject to lease 39 (if recorded)

-- triggers due-on-sale clause 375

-- pledge of rights in lease 278

leave of absence, notary, 72, 669

legal mortgage 286

legal regime (CP) 199

legacy 476; 3 types of 467; lapse of 492; examples 513; conjoint 477-79

legatee 480; ≠ heir 447

-- legatee/spouse as W 351, 482 (gets limited, but will valid)

-- notary as legatee 352, 482 (gets zero, but will valid)

-- after divorce 490, 510

legitime 484, 547 [*see* forced portion]

lesion 226; rescind partition 100

lessee (=renter), ch 14

lessor (=landlord), ch 14

liability of notary 75; fail to paraph 393

liability of parents aft emancipation 616

liberative prescription 76

licitation 99, 105, 123; of usufruct 105

life insurance: donate 149; trust 523; not part of estate 448

life-sustaining procedures, decl 351

lien examples: vendor's 370; private works act 608

limited emancipation (AA), 192, 616

limited jurisdiction ct, 24

'live birth' 180

living trust 524 (≠ inter vivos trust)

living will 488 (*not* health care POA 254, nor life-sust'g procedures 351)

lost original 612

low-profit LLC 593

major (age 18+), 169

maker 392, 623 (of prom. note/check)

malfeasance 47 (≠ *mis*feasance 75; unauth prac of law 76)

mandamus 305

mandatary (agent), ch 15

-- and servitudes 121

-- accepting d 134-35

-- can't make a will 253, 468; nor affidavit 367; nor marry 196, 253; nor adult adoption 603

-- putative mandatary (apparent authority) 259

mandate, health care 254

mandate 251-62

-- termination of 260 (by princ.), 261 (by agent)

-- compare procuration 250 (both are POA, 249)

manual gift of corporeal movable 148 (not AA; *but* OMV rule: 434, 644, 152)

marital portion 210; in trust 548

marital status, appearance clause, 340, 357

marital-status-change: 363; req'd: 342, 369, 385, 388; form: 363

marriage 195; legal impediments 196 (e.g. age, already married); covenant 197; name change aft 197

materialman's privilege or lien (similar to builder's lien, 608)

12 ▪ INDEX AND ADDITIONAL DEFINITIONS

matrimonial agreement (pre-nup), 209, 164; form & content, 617; 'duly acknowlg'd,' 329

maturity 391

measurements table 407

meridian 402

medical consent for child 618, 628

medical mandate (a POA) 254

meter

metes and bounds 408

military POA 31

minerals: rights 387, 292; mineral payment as pledge 279

minor 192; capacity to contract 168; donations 130; alienate prop of, 188, 191; emancipation of 192, 616; medical consent for 618, 628

'minute' (protocol/original), 9

missing person: dead?, 454

mobile home, immobilize 327, 387

modify inter vivos trust by a will 499

mortgage ch 18 & form: 387-92
 -- collateral m, 307-13
 -- m cancellation 299-305; compare extinction of m, 297
 -- m certificate 296
 -- m act, may have pledge in it, 279
 -- m, subordination of 632
 -- prop m can be used for 292, 299; but movables use UCC9: 292, 281
 -- special m 288-90; prop bond is, 66

mortgage records 295
 -- in >1 parish 296, 612
 -- maintain privacy of 398
 -- Orleans Parish 60, 354, 363
 -- recordation process/fees 354 [*see* rules under R]

mortgagee ch 18; defn., 287 (lender)

mortgagor ch 18, 287 (borrower)

mortis causa (will), ch 24, 129

movable 86, 89-90; donation of, 148
 -- act of sale for, ch 13
 -- titled vehicles, 426 & ch 23
 -- mortg not for 292, 281

name change: aft marriage, 197; aft adoption 186

name, full, 339, 469, 664 (*signature* can be less 347, 469)

nature: tutor by (natural tutor), 188; immovable by, 87; natural heir (would've inherited if no will) 489

naked owner 102

Napoleonic Code 17

ne varietur 621, 393
 -- no need if combine docs 313
 -- ne varietur note 308-11 (=collat'l mortg note)

non-alienation certificate

no-contest clause 493, 487

nonconsensual 170

nonconsummables 103

non-legal custodian's affid 618

non-resident

nominate contract 167

notary functions 54-55, 7, 9

notary qualifications 64; revoke / suspend comm'n 52-54, 665; liability 75, 393

notary as legatee 352, 482 (gets zero); as executor or trustee (OK), 351, 481

note 392, 310, 313; hand note 308-11

notice of lease 228-29

novation 246

NPI privacy 399

nullity: of acts in derogation 319

-- of contract 165, 174 (relative vs. absolute)

-- of donation 137-42 (grounds); 145 (abs. null if not AA), but confirm to cure, 146, 642, 174-76

-- of will w/o AA formalities 470, 636

oath 365; alternatives to swear, 344

obligation, ch 11; strictly personal 154, 260; proof of (< $500), 160

obligor/obligee 153

olographic will 468, 637; 'mark' isn't signature 348, 469; can't dispose of remains in 500

onerous donation 149-50, 132; onerous mandate 252; contract 168

online notary 698

option to repurchase (sale w/), 377

ordinary process (not executory) 298

order of signing (ptys → Ws → N) 346, 350, 638-42

'other valuable consideration,' 648

output contract 156

ownership in indivision 97, 91

Orleans Par. differs (incl 48 hrs to record): 60, 678, 682

-- doc transaction tax 354

-- for inventory 556

-- order of names, married couple 338

-- assumed business name 578

-- protest deputies 624 (bad checks)

-- attachments to acts 363

pact de non alienando 389

paiement, dation en, 380, 151

parishes (La. has 64), 57; parish courts 25

paraph 393, form for 621; cancel mortg 300

-- not needed if combine docs 313

-- use to link note & mortg 392

-- use to link partial release 393

partial release of mortgage 393; by financial inst., 301

particular legacy 467, 477, 513 n.12

partition: content & rules 621, 98

-- p by act inter vivos or will 498

-- p re usufruct 105; other servitudes 122

partition by licitation 99, 105, 123

partition: excluding it 98

-- rescinding it 100 (for lesion)

partition in kind 99, 123

partition of comm'ty prop 202

partnership 579-86; art's need not be Eng unless register 579

partnership in commendam 580

party wall 116

passage, right of 116

paternity, act acknowledg'g 599-602, 183

-- revoking that act 600 (both AA)

-- 'informal ackn' 184

patrimony (estate), 447, 465, 477; can't donate entire 137

pawn 274

payee 625

penalty clause in will 493, 487

per aversionem 407

perfection 283

perjury 333, 344, 366

per stirpes 457

personal servitude 101-12

person, defined 179 [*see* juridical pers.]

pet trust 525-27

pleadings, notary can't draft 321, 77

pleadings, verification of, 633

pledge ch 17
-- 2 modern examples of, 274
-- pledge of mineral payments 276

possession 90, 96, 213; 'possession is 9/10ths...' 96; quasi-possession 90-91

potestative 141, 156

pour-over trust 547

power of attorney 249 & ch 15
-- form for appearance clause 359; attachment to act 363
-- termination of 260; recordation req'd 261
-- death of principal 260; need to finish work 262
-- can't use for a will 253, 468; for affidavit 367; nor to marry 196
-- POA of titled vehicle 438

preemptive right (relates to ch 28)

precatory 507

predial servitudes 113-28

prescription (time limit) against notary 76

principal ch 15 (for POA sense): 251, 255; death of, 260, 262

principal (as in: trust prop), 517

principal contract 168

privacy, consumer (closing disclosures), 397-401

private act 328, 163 (=act under private signature)

private works act lien 608, 153

private act duly acknowledged 328, 330, 163; forms of ackn.: 359, 694

private trust 518

privilege, example: vendor's (credit sale), 370; ranking 371, 293, 632

proces verbal 553; form 558

procuration 250; oral or written 252
-- conditional, certify disability 251

promissory note 392, 148
-- as negotiable instrument, like check 392
-- secures collateral mortg 308, 310
-- in combined doc 314

property bond 65-67 (=special mortg)

property description ch 22; when req'd: 369, 372, 382, 385, 386, 388

property tax matters designee 63, 369, 372, 382, 385

protest 623; deputies, in Orleans 624

protho-notarial certif 626

protocol ('minute') 9

provisional custody by mandate 628

public adjuster license 344

public trust doctrine 84

putative mandatary 259

qualifications of notary 64

quitclaim 376
-- w/ right of redemption 379

ranking: incl rank of mortg's, 293,

632; & vendor's lien 370; subord. 632

real estate investm't trust (REIT) 527

'real right' defined 273, 154 (≠ real prop or real estate); real oblig'n 154

recapitulation 561

reconducted lease 245

recordation 353-56, 38, 59 [*can put whole topic at page top or at 'Q'*]

-- notary's duty relieved 60, 354

-- recordation req'd?, 353, 42, 59-61, 678; for d of immov? 152, 385, 42; 663; of credit sale 371

-- of mortgage 293, 295; of POA?, 261; of matrimonial agreement 618; to reserve fruits as SP, 201

-- notary's duty relieved 60, 354

-- not needed for security int in collat'l mortg, 354

-- prom note not filed 392; nor UCC9 sec interest, 283; but financing statement? 283

-- need to file for pledge of rights in lease 280

-- of trust instrument or extract 549

-- info required to record, list, 355

-- costs/fees borne by buyer 354

-- copying filed act 612 (by Clerk only); prop in 2 parishes 296, 612

reinscription 301, 280; or 'reviving' lien/mortg 301

release of obligee, partial 393, 302

remains of body, instruct on, 500-01; not by olographic 500; dead body not in estate 449

remote notary (RON), 698

remunerative donation, 150, 148

-- doesn't require AA, 148

-- repays services rendered 150

renunciation 452, 461 (by heir or legatee)

-- of predial servitude 127

-- of right to concur 203

-- of trust instrument by benef'y 541 (AA if inter vivos 542)

-- in favor of another (AA) 462

representation 456-58

representative ch 15 (also a 'representation'); appearance clause 359; succession represn'tive 450, 358

reservation of fruits of sep prop 201

retirement or leave of absence 72

restoration to donor 143

resolution, corp 394; appear by 359

resolutory condition 155,157; donor 136

resulting trust 527

restrictions, building 127

revoke/suspend notarial comm'n 52-54, 665

revoke: a mandate or POA 260; ackn. of paternity 600; donation 142

-- revoke: testament 483, 490, 509; a legacy in it, 510, 483; a trust, 531, 540

-- revoke/modify i.v. trust *in* a will 499; a usufruct in a will 489

right of way (of passage), 116 (a *predial* serv.)

right of use 112 (a *personal* serv.)

rule against perpetuities 555

sale per aversionem 407

sale, act of 368 (immov); bill of sale 434, 215 (mov)

sale w/ rt of redemption 377

school consent 618, 628

12 • INDEX AND ADDITIONAL DEFINITIONS

seal, signature is 74

section 404 (1/36th of township)

security agreem't, UCC9, 280-86; not a mortg if movable 292

-- part of collateral mortg package 308, 310

seizin 449, 514 n.16

self-employment tax 47

separate property 203; of deceased 458-62

-- fruits of SP are CP 201

-- describing it, in act 341

-- declar'n of acquisition of SP 201

separation, legal (spouse), 454 (if covenant marr.)

sequestration

servitude ch 9; personal serv 101-12; predial serv 113-28

-- extinguish it: 106, 489 (usufruct); 124 (predial)

servient estate: one so burdened, 113

settlor 517-18; revoke/modify trust in a will 499

'share and share alike' 477 (avoid)

signatures 346-51; on a will, 504; if olographic 466, 348

-- can't be a mark: olograph testator 469, 348; or W to notarial will 349

-- electronic signatures 350

-- notary's is her seal 74

siblings 453; none or half-, 459

simulations 147, 396, 172

small succession: see succ'n by affid

sole proprietorship 577-79, defined 576

social sec # (TIN), when req'd, 343, 396, 601; mortg 372, 388

small succession, ch 27 (< $125k)

special mortgage 288-90; as notary bond 66 (=prop bond)

special needs trust 525

specific legacy (=particular) 467, 477, 513 n.12

spouse: defined 195, 454; notarize for, 651; ex-spouse in will 490

-- surviving spouse's usufr 106, 458; modify it 489

spendthrift trust 543

stare decisis 34

statement of auth, 395, 598 (AA); but not AA: LLC certif of auth 395

Statutes, Revised ("R.S.") 30

statutory directives 62

strictly personal obligation 155, 110-11

subdivision 414

subordination 632

-- form for 633

-- for mortg, requires paraph 393, 633

subrogation 158-60 (e.g. successor pays expenses from own funds, 159)

subrogor/subrogee 158

substitution prohibited 140, 486, 136; vulgar sub OK 486, 513 n.15; condit'l legacy 491

succession ch 24; get car bef it opens 437

-- can't contract for 173

-- can't draft judicial one 564

succession by affid (small succ'n), ch 27

-- procedure/form 567

-- La. domiciliary, testate 569; domicile vs. residence 571

    -- movables vs. immovables 572

    -- notary duty to inform 574

supplemental needs trust 525

suppletive laws 319; donation 139

successors 447, 449; are heirs (intestate 453) or legatees (testate 480)

    -- if pay estate debts → gets subrogation, 159

    -- universal succ'r, accretion 479

    -- universal succ'r can confirm d 643

    -- unworthy succ'r (heir *or* legatee), 462, 497

supra

sui generis

summary proceedings 298

surety 263 (=guarantor)

  -- form req'd 264

suretyships, kinds of, 265; for notary, 65, 677

surviving spouse usufr 106, 458, 489

suspensive condition 155-57; donor 136

suspension of notary 52-54, 665

swear, alternative to 344, 345

tacit 146, 175

tactile interpreter 476

testament ch 24; notarial 470-514; olographic 468-70

testate 465

testator 465

testatrix 458

things, ch 8; defined 83

third person 487 (will may not give power to dispose; legatee isn't one)

third possessor 294

timber sale 383

TIN or social sec #, when req'd 343, 396, 601; mortg 372, 388

township 404

traverse 557 (challenge proces verbal)

trust ch 25; is not a juridical person 517, unless non-LA 518; but trust may be *for* a JP 529, 536; trustee is JP only if bank/trust co. 533; testamentary settlor not JP 530

  -- create by AA *or* ackn act 529, 329 (if done i.v.)

  -- modify/revoke in will 499, 531

  -- modify/revoke inter vivos? 531

  -- forced portion in trust 547

  -- term limits 544

  -- types of, 518-28

  -- pet trust 525

TRID, 397

trustee 517-18, 533

tutor 188, 615, 498; appear for minor 358

tutorship by will 498, 615, 190; or designate by AA 615

tutrix 189, 615

unauthorized practice of law, 76-79, 7

  -- pleadings 321

  -- penalties 78

  -- successions 564; trusts 521

unborn children 130, 179, 455

  -- as legatee 481; heirs differ 455

  -- as donee 130

undue influence 505, 170

unilateral contract 165, 167; procuration is, 250

universal legacy 467, 477, 513 n.14

universal successor 467, 477
  -- of the donor may confirm d 643
  -- accretion to, 479

Uniform Commercial Code 280

unworthy successor 462, 497

use, right of (personal serv), 112

usury

usufruct 102-10; may not in donation?, 132; surviv'g spouse 106, 458, modify by will 489, 106; jointly 459; legal vs. conventional 106

usufructuary 102 (who receives grant)
  -- may not establ servitude 121
  -- may lease 244
  -- pays HOA fees & prop tax 110

utilities, included in rt of passage 116

vendee 368

vendor 368

vendor's lien (privilege) in credit sale 370

vente a remere 377 (=sale w/ right of redemption)

venue 335

verification of pleadings/interrogs 633

virile share 579

voter registration by notary, 64; fix in 10 days 666

vulgar substitution (is OK), 486, 513 n.15; e.g. condit'l legacy 491

warranty, waiver of ("as is"), 648, 319

warranty deed (for cash sale), 368

warranty of [peaceful] poss'n 223

way, rt of (rt of passage), 116

will (testament), ch 24, 465

witness, 351-53; if legatee or spouse, 482, 351-52
  -- age of W: AA not a will 351; W to will 353, 481
  -- deaf or blind W to will 353, 481
  -- signature is mark 349 (not if will)

wrap-around mortgage (relates to ch 18)

Zamjahn case 346, 349, 639-42, 145

13

Cross-referencing Expanded

The study guide has a lot of cross-references built into it. That's good because it often splits information about one topic over two or more places. There's no real reason why they should detail emancipation on p. 192 and then provide the form to do it on p. 616. On the day of the exam you may need to consult both places, or more, to answer a question. That's especially so if my view is correct that they create many questions with the goal of making you look in both to figure out the answer. Even a straightforward question can have their desired level of difficulty if the answer combines parts of the book from different chapters, so you would not get it right glancing at the table of contents.

To that end, writing cross-references onto the pages to other subject-matter locations inside the text is nearly as important as annotating an index in back. At least the book already uses cross-references, and you may be able to get by with many of them as-is. There are two ways to improve it: First, use more cross-references than they already have. I offer several that seem to be missing in some testable areas, further below. You could add more as you study. You will probably use some of them on test day. If you don't find the answer in the place you've looked, go to the next location of that topic.

You can also quickly check the *index* entry for that subject to see if it lists two or more pages on the subject. If you expand the index completely as the previous chapter suggests, you may not need to add cross-references, though these page references do save time even if you index. If you decide not to have a complete index, adding references becomes essential. Remember to write in both (or more) places—back to each other—in print larger than their own examples.

Second, *paginate* the cross-references, even more than *Fundamentals* already does. This edition thankfully uses pages to reference, not just subject headings like older versions did. But be aware that they often take you to the first page of the general topic, while the specific point that's being referenced may be a few pages into that. You may want to pinpoint the actual page, as we do, if you see some of those along the way. And even where they have a cross-reference, write it big; this edition of the study guide unfortunately has removed some of the boldface they previously used for all cross-references.

We expand cross-references, below. We don't add cross-references to matter repeated in Appendix A's notary statute Title 35, though the most relevant and tested parts of it *are* indexed in our ch. 12. There are also several possible pinpoint cross-references within ch. 19 which could be added, not detailed here (though we have several); as disorganized as that chapter tends to be, there's still no substitute for reading it repeatedly. Ch. 24 and 25 could be cross-referenced somewhat more than is suggested here, too.

As with our index, what follows uses some abbreviations. And it often does not show the full range of pages for a topic, if the key page we list is enough since it's clear the discussion continues to the next page(s).

An example of specifically how to cross-reference in your book follows this list.

statutory duty to record 59 ←→ 353 notary duty, party direction, & req'd info

statutory directives for all acts/immovs 62 ←→ ch 19 acts & ch 21 transfers

bonds generally, and for notary 65 ←→ ch 16 suretyships and bonds

incorporeal movables defined 90 ←→ 148 donation of incorporeal movables

prop held in indivision 97 ←→ 621 partition by act ←→ 498 partition by will

usufruct: concept & rules 102 ←→ 458 usufr of surviving spouse of decedent ←→ 489 testator may modify/terminate usufr in a will

habitation is nonheritable 111 ←→ 155 so, it's a 'strictly personal obligation'

donation: concept & rules ch 10 ←→ 383 act of donation: form & content

donative intent words 131 ←→ 506 donative intent for donation *mortis causa* (will)

donation is irrevocable 132 ←→ 142 but 'ingratitude' allows revoking it ←→ 495 which is the same as ground to disinherit ←→ 483 revoking legacy

confirmation of donation 146 ←→ 642 confirming cures imperfect donation

donation in disguise 147 ←→ 645 cash sales, 'consideration,' & disguised donation

donation: manual gift of vehicle 148, 152 ←→ 434, 644 donation of titled mov.: AA?

dation en paiement 151 ←→ 380 form & content for act

acknowledged acts 163, 328 ←→ 332, 359 forms of acknowledgment ←→ 428 ackn on car title ←→ 635 ackn acts are "self-proving," but maybe not as to all parties

fetus as natural person 179 ←→ 481 fetus as legatee (but rule differs if no will)

domicile/residence 180, 571 ←→ 339 domicile clause in AA ←→ 614 decl to change

filiation and paternity 182 ←→ 600 ackn of paternity: form/content

tutorship 188 ←→ 498 appointing tutor in will ←→ 615 form for tutorship by will (designation of tutorship) ←→ 358 appearance clause when tutor appears for minor

emancipation of minor 192 ←→ 616 form for, is AA

community/separate prop 200 ←→ 458 community/separate prop in estate

matrimonial aprenup) agreement 208 ←→ 617 matrim'l agreemt form & content ←→ 329 valid only if acknowledgment or AA

power of attorney generally ch 15 ←→ 438 POA for vehicle transfer & at OMV

13 • CROSS-REFERENCING BY PAGE NUMBERS

mandatary/agent 252 ←→ 359 appearance clause when agent appears for principal

authority to donate must be express 253 ←→ 134 authority to *accept* need not be

UCC9 security agreem't 280 ←→ 310 combining it as part of collat'l mortg package

mortgage ch 18 ←→ 387 act: form/content ←→ 59 duty to record mortg

what a mortg may be used for 292 ←→ 281 mov's use UCC9, not mortg

appearance clause in AA 338 ←→ 340, 357 various forms for appearance clauses

'full name' in juridical acts 339 ←→ 441 odd name usages for car title

affidavits generally 333 (+ components 334) ←→ 361 form for affid ←→ 367 affid can't be done via agent

affidavit: content/form 334, 361 ←→ examples: ch 27 small succession; 439 & 603 acts of correction; 606 affid of distinction; 614 affid of custodian of orig records

'evidence of oath' forms 343 ←→ ch 20 oaths ←→ 361 oath in form affid

marital history 342 ←→ 363 m-status-change declr ←→ ch. 21 when req'd

conclusion of AA 345 ←→ 361 forms for conclusion (AA & affid) ←→ 470 attestation clause in will

signature of party 346 ←→ 347 what constitutes a signature of a party or witness? ←→ 505 testator's signature ←→ 469 olographic signature

affidavit 'sworn to and subscribed' 345 ←→ 616 is named 'jurat' & form

appearance of executor for estate 358 ←→ 450 succession administrator ←→ 490 executor

appearing for partnership, corp, or LLC 359 ←→ 576-77 those 3 entities ←→ corp resolution 394 (or LLC certif of auth 395) empowers someone to act for

incorporating other docs into act 362 ←→ 509 but different for will

requirement of paraph for note to mortg, vendor's lien, etc. 393 ←→ 621 forms for paraph/recitation of

affid of one & the same 440 ←→ 605 affid of distinction/of identity

accretion, lapsed or refused inheritance (intestate) 463 ←→ 478 lapsed legacy (testate) ←→ 541 accretion in trust law

capacity of testator 465 ←→ 503 determining testator capacity ←→ 481 who can be witness ←→ 320 capacity generally

signing olographic will (can't be mark) 469 ←→ 346 signatures generally ←→ 505 rules about signing both types of will

revocation of will or legacy 483 ←→ 490 revokes as to ex-spouse ←→ 509 revoking & modifying via codicil definition of forced heir/portion 484 ←→ 495 grounds (8) to disinherit ←→ 547 forced portion in trust

forms of trust (i.v. or will) 529 ←→ 132 no usufruct by donation? ←→ 546 donating prop to trust by AA ←→ 499 settlor may modify/revoke i.v. trust in a will

movables vs. immovables in small succ'n 572 ←→ 86 such things generally

non-legal custodian's affid 618 ←→ 628 provisional custody by mandate

AA not signed by all parties at same time 635-36 ←→ 162 using counterparts to sign separately

acts in foreign languages 655 ←→ 506 in will ←→ 586, 656 not in articles for corp or LLC ←→ 588 foreign language OK in corp/LLC *name* if English characters

How to cross-reference: The index (our ch. 12) should be written toward the back of the back (either in the glossary or separately). But these cross-reference entries belong *inside* the book, near various places of text. You can write them along the side margins at the precise location, or just at the top or bottom of a page. An example above is:

incorporeal movables defined 90 ←→ 148 donation of incorporeal movs

... which means for you to write, on p. 90, something like: "donation of incorporeal movables, 148" (without the quote marks—and use abbreviations you'll know). Then on p. 148, write: "incorporeal movables defined, 90." So, during the exam, if you're looking at one page, you can see that there is more information (especially a caution or exception, quite testable) about the same topic, or a closely related one, at another place of text—and vice versa.

14

Suggested Annotation Holes and Filling Them

These are places in the study guide where there's room for larger annotation beyond some marginal notes. In these places you can write out whole forms of commonly tested acts (donations, usufruct, power of attorney), add bulletpoint summaries of the law (e.g., class notes or notes/charts from other sources such as Michele's 2025 *Outline*), and have *lists* of certain rules that can be grouped together, with page numbers (see our ch. 15 below).

The obvious place to write notes and sample acts, and the lists we suggest in ch. 15, is the 16 blank pages entitled *Notes* at the back of the book as well as the inside cover to follow. We've already urged that they not be used up writing your index there (see ch. 12), as the index can be inserted efficiently into the glossary it already has. Of course the index *can* go onto the blank pages (and pretty much has to, if you have big handwriting). But that space is better reserved for more extensive outlining and lists, charts to help answer predictable questions, and possibly writing out some of the most testable acts, as discussed below.

If the blank pages fill up with an index or notes, you may need more places in the book to take notes or write out acts. Or you may want some of the lists and bulletpoint notes to fit closer to the pages where the actual topic comes up, so they're easily seen with the relevant text on exam day. Either way, there's still a place for finding blank spots in the book or turning some pages of text into blank ones using white-out.

You're reclaiming real estate in the book to be able to write more info useful on test day. These tips are not so much about saving time beforehand—it admittedly takes work to create new blank paper and fill it with new material—as about maximizing the chance of passing. And that means being able to quickly see, during the exam, the most common topics you've organized before the exam. Plus the very act of writing acts or notes into your guide is enormously *engaged* studying that should pay off.

The blank pages (or parts of pages) fall into two camps, depending on how ambitious you are with this concept. First, areas already blank, ready to be annotated—beyond the 16 sides in back. These are visually obvious, so I won't belabor it, other than to share some ideas as to what can fill the space usefully. The ideas are not meant to be exhaustive but just point you in the direction you could take it yourself.

Second, areas in the guide ideal for whiting out, to create room for more notes and sample acts to have handy. This takes more time but creates more room to do more. Don't lay the liquid paper on too thick; just paint a layer, let it dry, then repeat. Use a non-gel pen over the new white space.

If you do write in notes and acts into your book, be sure to add the page reference to your expanded index. You have to be able to access the samples on exam day. Seeing an actual document for that type of legal act will make their library document—often full of errors and missing parts—stand out by comparison, letting you ID the mistakes and holes.

Before offering some possibilities of items to copy or create in the study guide, let me stress the *essential* one: a general form for most *authentic acts*. Writing this exemplar out by hand is a necessary part of studying, and having it readily accessed during the exam helps answer questions. This is especially so if they, as they often do, give part of a library document of some act they want you to consider and know its features and flaws. For that, having a viable comparison is crucial. They already do this for you with the *will*: pp. 512-14 and its footnotes provide a good sample. *You* need to do this for the other version of an authentic act, applicable to all sorts of instruments and situations.

The general components list they give you in ch. 19 is confusing because it also includes parts of an affidavit. It also doesn't explain the parts there. It's better that you write out the key and distinctive parts of the typical authentic act and insert some sample phrasing such an act would have for preamble, appearances, conclusion, signatures, etc.

Our ch. 8 has the skeleton of a valid authentic act, with some notes on each bone. At the very least, *that* checklist needs to be written as a handy part of your guide. In addition, you could write out nearby a specific, complete example of an authentic act—such as an Act of Donation of Immovable (a good example, but quite involved) or an Act of Adult Adoption—to illustrate how the bones can be given flesh in a specific context. The one you pick may well be one that gets tested; but even if not, it's a useful example of how such acts are constructed.

To me, the best place to add the outline of components from ch. 8 is the page facing the inside back cover. It's handy on exam day, needs no index to find it, and has plenty of room to write the basic form and notes—such as cross-references, variations, and sample specific language (e.g., an appearance clause if it were a limited emancipation or a mortgage with a confession of judgment). Then there's more room on the opposite page (the actual inside back cover) to insert a filled-out example of an authentic act. We provide a sample donation in our ch. 18. Of course one of the Notes pages could be used for this outline and sample, but it fits nicely at the end of the book and would be the act you access the most on test day.

Besides the act of donation, the *second* most important instrument to think about, if not write out, isn't necessarily an authentic act but does get tested: an Act of Usufruct—assuming you did insert the donation above, which is more testable. That act—or notes about its components at least—could fit well on the inside *front* cover and, if necessary, its facing page (on which you've created room by white-out). Whether this act must be authentic turns on whether it's donating versus selling the interest.

The *third* most important form to consider may be the power of attorney. Near the back of the book (at pp. 736-37 whited out), new space could be used for a sample mandate. Another possible place, at the front, would be pp. ii-iv. We provide a sample power of attorney in ch. 18.

For any of the above, the main takeaway—and the main thing to consider actually writing into the book—is the appearance clause. They do routinely test on your understanding of how these are structured, from ch. 19, especially for married appearers or parties appearing in a representative capacity.

Somewhere on this list of top three or four, you may have already inserted a sample affidavit near (or into) the "form" in ch. 19. We discussed this in our ch. 7. Adding a short one, like our affidavit of translation in our ch. 18, will be instructive. Knowing the different parts of an affidavit, as opposed to most other acts, is likely to be tested on exam day—answered easily with a visual example. Again, though, it's the exercise of writing a sample affidavit somewhere, if not the study guide, that forces you to know components like evidence of oath and the jurat.

I'd say the three or four above are the minimum forms to add, for real help on the exam. True, the exam is evolving into one with fewer long library documents and more standalone scenarios. So it would seem that the traditional method of instruction making you write out lots of acts is not as crucial as it was for previous exams. Still, it's easy to construct scenarios that test your understanding of the different acts, their components, appearance clauses, and who signs in what capacity. Some of these will be based on clauses of acts they show above the question, if no longer a separate file of library documents.

The studying sweet spot, in my opinion, is no longer extensively creating acts in the study guide as if that directly is tested anymore, but still going through the process of writing some sample components enough that you can answer questions about them. Definitely look over our ch. 18 and see how these common forms are constructed.

You may also want to use free space to write in charts of the differences between various transfers of land (cash sale vs. credit sale vs. bond for deed, etc.), or of the typical order of succession that occurs in an intestate succession. Michele's *Outline* has several useful charts to add to your guide.

I've already advised painting room for some sample form at the front, opposite the inside front cover, or using pp. ii-iv. Already-blank space includes half or all of pp. xxx, 18, 20, 37, 80, 100, 152, 211, 248, 286, 314-15, 401, 445, 515, 551, 563, 574, and 657. Other areas in the book that can disappear by white-out (without your missing anything) are suggested below.

- v through x
- 3, 4 (even 1 and 2 once read, if needed)

- 12 (half-blank and easily made fully so)
- 21
- 81
- 316 (making three pages in a row)
- 658, 659 (making three in a row)
- 736, 737 (noted above)

15

Useful Lists to Insert into the Guide

Without trying to be comprehensive in all the bulletpoints one could insert into the guide as notes, this chapter does suggest some key lists that pull together rules or law spread over many places in the book. For example, you saw one such list at the end of our "Acts Required to be in Authentic Form" in ch. 9, and detailed below: four situations in which a power of attorney cannot be used. Rather than indexing the four different places in the book saying this, write all four in one place—anywhere—then index just that (as "power of attorney can't be used for, p. xxx,"; also add "mandate can't be used for, p. xxx"). Of course the section on required authentic acts is itself a list compiled from all through the book.

Here are similar useful lists to write somewhere. I also suggest where to write them (matching the index entry), but anywhere is fine as long as you can find it.

1. <u>Situations when social security number or TIN is required</u> as part of appearance clause or similar (p. 343).

7 docs require SS#; use last 4 digits of *borrower*/mortgagor (or full EIN if juridical person), for our first 4 here:

    1) conventional mortg

    2) collateral mortg

    3) credit sale (buyer=mortg'or)

    4) any doc creating secur. int. in immov

       + 3 docs use full #:

    5) TIN of juridical persons in Art. of Incorp. or similar SOS filing

    6) SS# of each parent in act acknow'g paternity, p. 601

    7) TIN of Unincorp. Ass'n in Statement of Authority, p. 396
       [include my page references in list]

2. <u>Situations when a paraph is required</u> (p. 621); but paraph actually goes on Note, see below.

    1) mortg (conv., collat., etc.); but parties have power to direct Notary not to

    2) sale with mortg

    3) credit sale

4) pledge

5) act of partial release

6) act of subordination (p. 633)

These require notary to place the *paraph* (starts with "Ne varietur," p. 621) on the <u>Note</u>, identifying it with a transaction. It's a 2-way street (p. 393), requiring "*recitation of paraph*" ("And I," p. 621) on mortgage, etc. For paraphing the promissory note itself, see p. 392 ("may be paraphed"—but notary never *signs* note). [I suggest writing this paragraph with the list.]

3. <u>When a mandate or power of attorney cannot be used</u>.

We suggest adding this to the top of p. 249 close to its introduction on power of attorney. Or you can add index entries like "power of atty, can't be used for." (I suspect relinquishing or acknowledging paternity should be on the list, too, but the study guide doesn't say.)

4 things can't be done by POA:

1) testament

2) affidavit

3) marriage

4) adult adoption

4. <u>Recordation rules; Orleans exceptions</u>.

This is done in our suggested index itself (ch. 12 above). Even if you don't insert an index in such detail as this book advises, at least collect all the settings and rules for recordation and filing of acts and other legal instruments (so, write our Recordation entries and page numbers somewhere into the study guide). Same with *Orleans Parish differences* (on recording and more): it's quite testable to place a scenario in New Orleans and so make one question turn on the differences that are not found in just one place in the guide. So at least index all pages that distinguish Orleans practice (see our index, ch. 12, under Orleans).

5. <u>When usufructs terminate</u> (pp. 106-07).

1) at death of usufructuary (natural person)

2) at remarriage (surviving spouse), ordinarily [but testator can extend]

3) when grant says so, if earlier than death

4) in 30 yrs or end of juridical person (if juridical person)

6. <u>Common reasons a notarial testament can or will be declared invalid</u>.

- Improper form
- Lack of capacity of testator

15 • USEFUL LISTS TO INSERT

- Representative or agent executed testament
- Two testators on same will
- Bottom of each page not signed by testator (even if double-sided)
- Improper attestation clause (incl. wrong one for blind, deaf, illiterate, etc.)
- Attestation clause not individual to testator
- No date (or uncertain/inconsistent dates that can't be fixed by extrinsic evidence)
- Designating a 3rd party power to dispose of property
- Testament written in language not understood by all involved
- Improper witnesses (e.g., under 16; or blind; or deaf but only if testator is blind or illiterate); but not necessarily that W is spouse, legatee, or notary
- Signed in improper order: must be T → Ws → N
- Witness not present at signing by testator[*]

7. <u>Common situations in which marital status of parties is to be given.</u>
   - Authentic acts involving immovables
   - Act of Limited Emancipation
   - Act of Cash Sale
   - Affidavit of Small Succession
   - Donation inter vivos
   - Mandate
   - Provisional Custody by Mandate
   - Testament[†]

---

[*] List of reasons a notarial will fails is based on one generously shared with permission of Kristy Ponevelle.

[†] List of situations requiring parties' marital status is generously shared with permission of Denise Turbinton, *citing* Title 35, § 11; and https://legis.la.gov/legis/law.aspx?d=92594; *see also* https://legis.la.gov/legis/LawSearchList.aspx. In addition to the above main examples, current marital status is expected in any act where knowing their status is important to giving context to whatever is being done in the act. For instance: if it's important to know whether the mortgagor is married, whether the adopted adult has a spouse who must consent, who the spouse is in a will, etc. So, other examples would be credit sale or other property transfers (including exchange, dation, or quitclaim—or even granting a usufruct, as conveying an interest in immovables), a judgment-creditor affidavit made under R.S. 9:5501.1, a mortgage, and an act of adult adoption (where the spouses, if any, appear ["intervene"] to approve).

Note that this is not the same as the situations in which a *change* in marital-status clause (change or no-change statement) must be included, often in property deals. The main context requiring that additional information is when a property or interest in a property is being

8. Authentic acts that also use affidavit form and have components of an affidavit, especially "evidence of oath" and "jurat." This is discussed below in ch. 16, including possible places to list them in your study guide.

9. Effect of divorce. Here is a list (including page cites and CC articles) of very testable situations (e.g., multiple questions on the September 2023 exam). A question may ask, in some form: Unless otherwise stated by the party, *does divorce terminate the following? Yes or No.* (Meaning, does the relationship or status end when the marriage does?)

1. POA agency appointment – No: pp. 260-61, arts. 3024-3026 (divorce not listed as grounds for termination)

2. legacy in a will – Yes: p. 490, art. 1608(5)

3. appointment as executor, trustee, or attorney for estate in a will – Yes: p. 509, art. 1608(5)

4. the community (the legal regime) – Yes: p. 206, art. 2356

5. sole proprietorship – Yes: p. 576, art. 2356, to the extent it was in legal regime

6. parental authority – Yes: p. 188, art. 235

7. provisions in testamentary trust appointing now-former spouse – Yes: p. 493, art. 1608(5)

8. inter vivos trust appointing or designating now-ex – Yes: p. 532, R.S. 9:2047

9. emancipation of a minor obtained by marriage – No: p. 192 art. 367

10. willingness to give up that plaid EZ Chair – Yes, but ratty plaid chair *should* be at curb

Write this list (except #10) into your study guide, somewhere easy to find during the exam. Perhaps in your added index under "Divorce," say where this list is (Divorce: terminates status? list: p. ___).

---

transferred (sold, donated, exchanged, etc.), then the transfer<u>or</u>'s change or no-change status since first acquiring property must be included. Why? Because the transferor can only transfer what they own, and we don't really know what they own unless we know their marital status *and* what it was when the property interest was first acquired. And for this we only care about it for the transferor, not the donee, buyer, or other transferee (recipient).

16

Ambiguities in the Study Guide

The following are areas of the study guide which may be ambiguous or worded confusingly. Or subject matters where the book seems to leave open a definitive rule. In these instances I provide my best guess below as to how to deal with the issue if it's tested, short of "challenging" a question for asking a question to which the study guide gives two answers (they do allow you to challenge questions by a note you include with your answers, though it's not clear it's worth the time). The good news is that they probably won't test on areas where the authors may have realized they were vague on the point. But these are food for thought.

What's in a name? Really, how *full* does it have to be? The notary statute R.S. 35:12(2) (see p. 649) says acts require a "full name." But lots of formats really qualify, as the statute makes clear. One that always *fails* is initials-plus-last, and they're most likely to test that (e.g., in the context of a will or other authentic act). So, *you can't use J.W. Booth.* Nor can you just use Wilkes Booth, even if he goes by his middle name (as I do). But it's also clear that these are all fine: John Wilkes Booth; John W. Booth; or J. Wilkes Booth (yes, *that's* a full name). Realistically, even John Booth should be enough—probably so in real life, and many exemplars use just two names in their sample forms; but one *could* read Title 35 as requiring that an initial be included if the signer has one.

Signature uses initials instead of writing out full name. Actually, using a full name, above, is not the same as how "full" their *signature* has to be written, which can be quite truncated or illegible (p. 347 of study guide). There's no intended ambiguity here. But it's easy for a student to get "name" mixed up with "signature." Those are really two different components of an act or instrument. Even a "mark" as signature is enough, if intended to act as signing—except for signers of olographic wills (p. 348) and witnesses to a notarial one (p. 349).

Can you use 'Sr.' in a name on an act? Technically, the answer should be "no," since that adds information that is not on the signer's driver's license. Certainly it's "no" for a certificate of title, which needs to track the license exactly (p. 441). In reality, people want them on a will or the like to differentiate their son or grandson, and there seems to be no harm (in fact, clarity is always better). But the exam answer would appear to be "no" in many contexts.

How old does a witness have to be? The general answer seems to be old and mature enough to understand the importance of what it going on (p. 351). That is not much guidance and is a judgment call in practice (but why risk making an act invalid by assuming a kid has "proper understanding"?). It's certainly true, and testable, that the age for a witness to a *will* is fixed by statute and laid out on p. 353. But for non-will situations, my suggestion is to use the general analysis on p. 351 and don't go too low in age unless the facts they give you in a scenario spell out that a minor is mature enough to have proper understanding.

What part of the authentic act is the "evidence of oath" mentioned in chapter 19 at p. 343? For most authentic acts *by far*, it's *not* a part, and really should not be discussed at this point of the book. It's also a bit confusing or cluttered to list it as a component of "juridical acts" on p. 335 in a chapter where they're talking mainly about authentic acts. In reality, "evidence of oath" is a component of affidavits and verifications, pp. 334, 361 (statement of being duly sworn). The reason the book mentions it there in ch. 19 is either because they're trying to be global/generic in talking about all notarial acts, even those not authentic (mainly affidavits), or because there *are* a few authentic acts in the form of affidavits, for which a component is the evidence of oath introduction, and the closing jurat. Examples of hybrid authentic acts/affidavits—not called "authentic affidavits" but you can think of them that way—are:

- *Act of correction (for immovable).* Either by notary or sometimes by parties. See pp. 603-05. Though the guide insists this is an authentic act and not an affidavit, it also notes that the original notary appears as an affiant and affirms the fact of his error. It could be done with evidence of oath plus jurat, but with all the ritual and two witnesses of authentic acts generally. Conceptually, it's an affidavit but in authentic form.

- *Affidavit of immobilization of a movable.* See p. 87, discussing this act as a "declaration" but not quite mentioning that it's often an affidavit and that it may have to be authentic, too. (Compare p. 387 re mobile homes.) Out of caution, in practice one would make the follow-up act of *de*immobilization, p. 87, also in authentic form. But it would appear that the exam answer for *de*immobilization via an act that ordinarily would not be AA, such as a cash sale, is that it need not be authentic.

- *Declaration of dispensation from collation?* This is mentioned on p. 326 as requiring authentic form. It's also likely required to be in the form of a valid affidavit, with evidence of oath and jurat. Out of caution, you should certainly construct it that way in practice, and answer any question as though this declaration is, in effect, an authentic affidavit.

Anyway, you may make a note at p. 335 to save "evidence of oath" only for those instruments requiring an oath, and list the above uncommon hybrids there.

Small succession affidavits (ch. 27) are often written in the form of a true affidavit, though with multiple signers, and then they include evidence of oath and jurat. But they can also be authentic acts that expressly state that the signers understand that they make the representations under penalty of perjury. In practice, it's common to make it a formal affidavit (adding the required perjury clause), and also have two witnesses sign it. The goal is to get it honored by banks, OMV, etc., who may be looking for it to be not only in affidavit form but witnessed. But the *exam answer* is that small successions are not required to be authentic acts and thus do not *require* two witnesses to the signing.

Does my home parish have reciprocal jurisdiction with one close by? It doesn't matter—unless you're already a notary who got your commission before June 2005. The whole ch. 7 discussion (and map and tables) of parishes, groupings, and small-population allowances (pp. 56-58) is only applicable to pre-2005 notaries. Yet the way it's introduced (notaries "may only execute their acts within the limits of their jurisdiction," followed by parish groups of "jurisdictional limits") makes every reader think new notaries can only work in limited parishes or parish groups. But a few pages later the book subtly states that those who take and pass the notary exam (so, *every* exam-taker since mid-2005!) have *state-wide* jurisdiction. So, you will be able to notarize anywhere in the state, as can lawyer-notaries. The only ones who cannot, and for whom the pages of info on groups and adjacent parishes count at all, received their commission a long time ago and never took the SOS exam after. The older rules are testable, since they're in the book, but they confuse my students consistently. It should *start* with a warning that this limited-jurisdiction section is superseded for new notaries.

What is "heritable"? A section clarifies that it doesn't mean "inheritable" (given after death) but rather "able to be transferred" (p. 154). But elsewhere it's used to mean "inheritable," as when a usufructuary is allowed to sell, encumber, or transfer his interest (p. 102), so transferable, but it's "not heritable" (pp. 111-12). This, in contrast to the right of habitation, which is neither (p. 111). Anyway, use the term generally as defined on p. 154. But in a specific context, don't rely on the word itself as meaningful shorthand; go to the place in the book and answer the question based on the details you find there: make a marginal note as to whether that right, property, or interest is (1) able to be transferred by the holder during her lifetime (also called "alienable"), and (2) able to be passed to an heir or legatee vs. it ends at the holder's death. E.g., a donee must accept while alive.

Where to file a matrimonial agreement? P. 603 suggests that it is recorded in each parish where the property is located *and* in the parish of matrimonial domicile. But really that's dependent on whether the property is movable or immovable, as the quoted code article makes clear. Make a note in the margin to read and apply the code article if they ask a filing question (I'd put a question mark on "and"). A clearer statement of the rule can be cross-referenced to p. 211.

Another ambiguity for such marriage agreements is whether they are valid if executed after the wedding. Generally not, to opt out of the legal regime (hence, "pre-nup"), unless the couple goes to court (or they moved into Louisiana and have a year to opt out). But a sentence on p. 210 sounds like it has to be done before marriage with a notary only if using the acknowledgment process, as opposed to authentic form. No, either way, it has to completed before the marriage begins. The study guide also emphasizes that doing this by the acknowledgment process requires that *both* spouses go to the notary to acknowledge it (unlike most forms of acknowledgment which are done by one party or a witness).

Is an acknowledged act "self-proving"? Yes, as is eventually made clear, at p. 635. That means that it is adequate proof, just on paper, of what it purports to be—without requiring a witness in court to support it (same with an authentic act). The short and traditional way of saying that is calling it "self-proving," and previous editions used that phrasing in many places. They don't say that as much anymore. But you should know that, in other places, the study guide means the same thing when it says that acknowledged acts (like authentic ones) "shall be admitted in evidence without further proof" (p. 330). So, in the margin, I write "self-proving" and cross-reference p. 635. This quality stands in contrast to mere acts under private signature, which require courtroom proof (p. 328).

BTW, occasionally in the book, in this context and others, the authors refer to "extrinsic evidence." Generally, that just means external to—outside of—the acknowledged or authentic act. Mere private acts need courtroom (extrinsic) proof. The terms of most contracts cannot be countered by extrinsic evidence.

Errata sheets on the SOS website. You can (and should regularly) access these ahead of the exam and correct or complete your study guide from that. They tend to locate a link to a PDF of the current errata sheet at the subpage "Prepare for the Notary Exam." They'll consider it fair game for testing even if it's not actually in the printed guide. They do not allow you to insert loose pages—even of their own errata sheets. Go ahead and *write* notes of the errata directly into the textbook, *before* the exam day, to have them available. They may also hand you the errata sheet at the test site, but you don't want to be reading these on the fly at that time—and *especially* don't copy them into your book in the test room (before or after the exam starts), violating their rules and risking dismissal.

Is a deaf person eligible to witness a will? Yes, unless it's a relatively rare will made under special provisions (art. 1579) for a testator who is blind or illiterate. The study guide says (p. 482) a deaf person "cannot be a witness to a notarial testament under Article 1579." This would be clearer if they said "only to a testament *that is made specially* under Article 1579."

Is the phrase "I give" a clear enough expression of donative intent? No, for a donation inter vivos—but yes, for a will. P. 132 seems to approve "I give/grant/ transfer/convey" even for inter vivos gifts, but they mean that's OK when coupled with the first part of the sentence, "out of love and affection...." Instead, clearer terms include "I gift" or "I donate." They test on this often, yet Facebook posters consistently insist they quoted "I give" right out of the study guide. True, but the question they were asked was missing the "love" set-up that makes it clear this is not a loan or a mere wish.

May a null donation be confirmed after the donor has died? Yes, by the universal successor, even tacitly (p. 147), or before death by donor in an AA (p. 146). This *seems* inconsistent with p. 175: there's no "confirmation in any manner of a donation mortis causa." But the latter refers to a will, in which it's too late for anyone to undo an invalid will, whereas p. 147 means a donation made while donor was still alive, but failed for form, then confirmed after donor dies.

17

Visualizing Community Property and Wills

The study guide's organization is a bit daunting on the issues raised by wills, successions, and property ownership. There's no real big picture given, so that in ch. 8 you're studying what "things" are, then ch. 12 says how married people own property in Louisiana. There's a little more on marriage agreements in ch. 12 and also 29, then the big payoff in ch. 24: how this affects inheritance (if intestate) or legacies (testate) in a court succession—what other states call "probate." It also affects how small successions work, ch. 27, especially the initial tally of the estate to see whether it's small enough to qualify for succession by affidavit—without court. That's a lot of property-wills-successions spread over six chapters!

Stepping back, the main takeaway is that a succession (whether in court or by affidavit) has to deal with, and finalize the transfers from, the decedent's estate. And that depends on what the "estate" is, which—before that, even—turned on what the decedent "owned" before she or he died. So, the concept of ownership matters, not just when the decedent was alive, but also in sorting it out after. The main reason the study guide explains ownership in detail early in the book is not because of how the person owns while alive, but more for what she or he owns—sum total—at the moment of death. That adds up to the "estate," which then becomes a matter for a succession to sort out.

(Well, OK, owning property in community or separately could also matter for donations *inter vivos*, since you can't give what you don't own. You do learn ch. 12's community property law also for the chance that it affects such a donation. But on the exam, property ownership comes up more with testamentary dispositions—the donation *mortis causa*—or as its own set of questions.)

The post-mortem sorting out can be done by operation of law—by the default rules applied to those who died *intestate*—or can be controlled by the decedent in advance via a will (a/k/a testament, essentially a donation that kicks in at the moment of death, instead of immediately like with donation *inter vivos*). Having a will gives the decedent not only control over the division of property through succession—perhaps deviating from the default rules (intestate) of who gets what—but also control over small but important extras that intestate law doesn't deal with at all: naming a tutor for kids, naming an executor to help run the whole thing till the succession is closed, creating trusts for the benefits of others, and even dealing with your body's remains (at least with a notarial will). So, it's a good idea to leave a testament, not only to specify who-gets-what.

Louisiana testators can do this in two ways: with an *olographic* will, or a *notarial* one. Even those written by attorneys are "notarial" in the sense that they become real once notarized, whoever drafted it. Guess which version involves the notary. Guess which is most likely tested (and most complicated, so there's more to test). This chapter will be about the notarial will, more than the olographic one or even the default inheritance rules for those without a will—though lots of notarial-will law turns on details of the intestate succession, too.

So, before learning the content and rules for a notarial will, you need to understand the property system. In particular, Louisiana and several other states use community property law (the "legal regime") to govern ownership of things during life and—for our purposes, more importantly—at death. During the marriage, they have much of their property owned together in the sense that they live "in a community of acquets and gains." They may each own separate property, too, according to detailed rules about property that's owned separately while otherwise the couple lives in community and shares much ownership. Even couples that live "in community" may have *some* property that is separate This is quite apart from a matrimonial agreement that lets them opt out completely of the "legal regime," p. 199, so that they'd be in a "contractual regime" (all separate).

The following is of course oversimplified, but it does present the big picture (literally), leaving many details to the study guide. And many others it omits are important for successions in court, or dealing with community property in life, but are not particularly handled by notaries and not tested on the exam.

Our discussion will assume, for clarity's sake and not because it's necessary, a husband and wife where the husband dies first. They *didn't* opt fully out of the community property system, and they each have some separate property *and* share in the community for many other belongings, both movable and immovable. They have children, perhaps under 24 or otherwise subject to the rules of forced heirship—who won't be entirely cut out of inheriting (no matter how the will's gifts are written). And we assume the husband does have a valid notarial will (maybe the wife does, too, but it doesn't matter in our illustration, since *he* died). His death immediately puts law into action (by *seizin*, p. 449).

Had he died intestate, all sorts of default rules would control. Many of the same concepts of property ownership and what's in the estate, as discussed below, would apply to his intestate succession, too, mainly differing in *who* must get the estate. But it does get more complicated since he has a will, partly because he may have redirected his gifts away from the default recipients. This is because the law of *forced heirship*, unique to Louisiana among the 50 states, limits his discretion in how much he'll actually "redirect" away from some kids who would've been heirs if he'd died intestate. He doesn't have *complete* control, but way more than he'd have if he had no will at all. He's Adam, and she's Eve.

With that in mind, think of the L-shaped state of Louisiana as made up of three squares. The three also form a rectangle vertically and another one horizontally. For this state, that's a North-South rectangle on the West side, and an East-West rectangle to the South. Mississippi is not part of the equation.

17 • VISUALIZING COMMUNITY PROPERTY AND WILLS

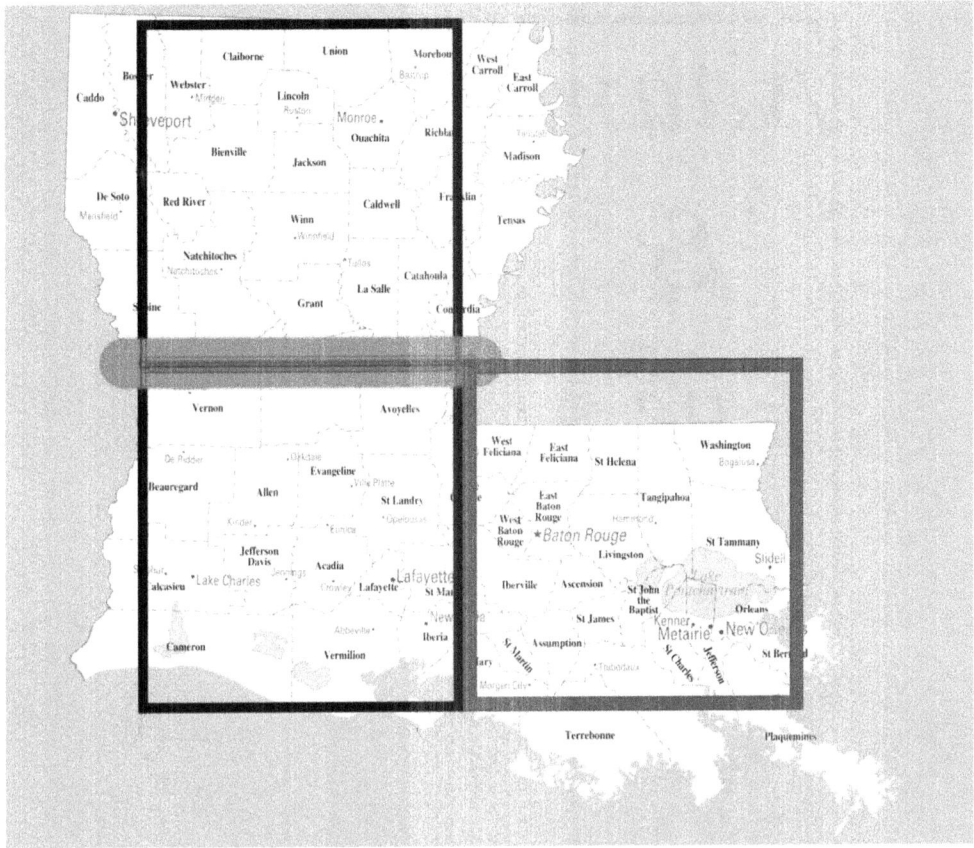

Fig. 1: Our state is an L with 3 boxes (or is it 2 rectangles?)

That's the visual. Then there are two important moments in time: while married and Adam's still alive; and at the moment Adam dies. He had executed the will (and the notary "received" it) before he died. But the succession has to divvy up his estate sometime after his death, following the dictates of the will to the extent they followed the law.

The notary's job was to write a valid will expressing the testator Adam's wishes for that moment. The notary needs to understand how property works to implement those wishes. We'll leave it to the succession, usually in court and without a notary's help, to sort out lots more details to finalize the disbursement. For purposes of the exam, the key is to know the law enough to express those wishes validly and to know notary practice enough to write the will competently. Ch. 10, above, was mainly about that drafting task, and that's tested a lot, too. This chapter is about the law of notarial wills that operationalizes the wishes.

Let's start with the time when they were both alive and owned property—lots of it even owned "together."

Fig. 2: While they're alive and married

Much of the property they own is actually held in community. It's like it's its own thing, though the book stresses it is not a juridical person. It's just a combo of their interests for their "community property." It's shown here as a large swatch of the state, though of course their community property could be a small part of what they each own. But it's a fair characterization because many married couples have, mostly, community property. Each spouse then "owns a present undivided one-half interest in the community property" under the Civil Code (p. 202).

To help visualize this further, and perhaps for you to draw onto p. 57's own state map to have during the exam, note that *all* of the parishes that begin with *C* are in or near the western/left side of the state: the community rectangle extends "geographically" from Caddo and the Carrolls at the top, down through many other *C* parishes like Caldwell and Concordia, all the way south to Calcasieu and Cameron. There are plenty more ***C* parishes** in that rectangular area, too. But there are zero *C* parishes in the southeast corner outside of it.

Adam and Eve hold community property together while married. ***CP*, like Claiborne Parish or Catahoula Parish, or those many other *C* Parishes.**

17 • VISUALIZING COMMUNITY PROPERTY AND WILLS

Fig. 3: Also while they're married, Adam has some SP

Adam also had some separate property when he was alive and married (not by opting out of the legal regime, but by owning some individually while *also* sharing in the community). He may have inherited a $10,000 Rolex from his uncle, or owned a house before they married that he kept as separate property (and has not "commingled" the two kinds of property enough to lose its "separateness"). Eve may have donated her interest in a piece of community property to him, making it separate, p. 206. However it happened, assume that he does own some separate property. It may not be as proportional a part of his total-ownership as the above shows. It could be a big or small part of his total assets. We'll assume the above is accurate enough in this case. It's *in addition to* that big CP rectangle.

By the way, Eve may have some separate property, too. It might be all of Arkansas, for all we know. It's not really taken into account in the testable part of what happens when *Adam* dies, though. So, ignore the fact that she may really own way more than him, or way more than a half-interest in the CP rectangle. Arkansas is big, but it's Adam's SP that we're concerned with.

Note that almost all of the **nine** (!) parishes that start with *S* are in the southeast quadrant of the state. They start with a "Saint" (Ignore St. Landry, please.) They are the **S Parishes. And where the Saints Play. *SP*, like separate property.**

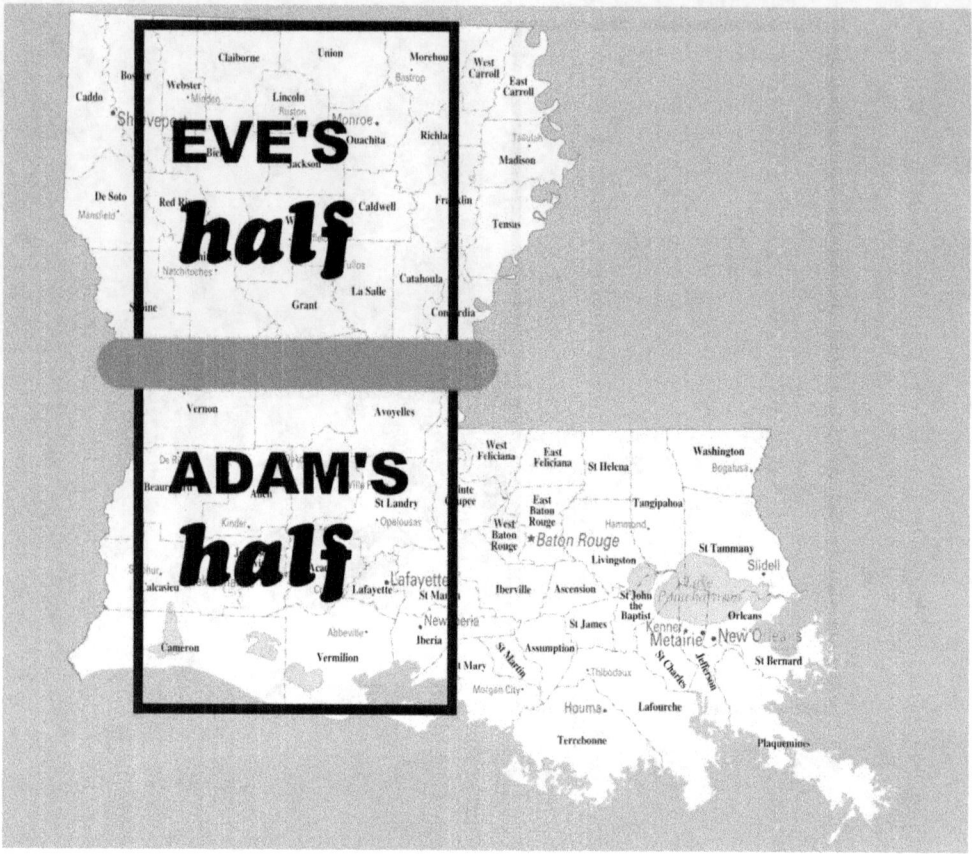

Fig. 4: When Adam dies

At the exact moment of Adam's sad death from apple poisoning, *the community terminates*. What used to be community property is now seen as each spouse now owning half of *ex*-CP. It's not just a half-interest in the whole anymore. It's two separate squares of property now. Eve now owns her half outright.

Assume Eve didn't kill him—assume the bad apple came from some other source. Otherwise, she is an "unworthy successor," to the extent she's a successor at all, p. 462. That would change a lot of the rules, unless he forgave her (for an attempt).

Most people think that the surviving spouse is naturally an heir or legatee. Usually not. Follow the rules in ch. 24 as to lines of inheritance to get this. But of course, up to a point, Adam could've provided in his will that she receives his property.

When he dies, his half of the ex-CP property is part of his *estate*. One may describe people as having an estate before they die, of course, and it would've included his *interest* in the CP, but it's when he dies that we care, for test purposes, what's in his "estate." Here, that estate includes his half-share of what used to be CP.

Importantly, *his* estate does not include *Eve's* SP or, more tested, her half of the community that is now part of her own total-ownership we might call *her* estate.

17 • VISUALIZING COMMUNITY PROPERTY AND WILLS

Fig. 5: His whole estate also includes his SP

At the moment of Adam's death, his estate not only consists of his half of the ex-CP property, but also his separate property. His estate could include half of a hunting camp that used to be CP, half a car, and savings they shared—but also SP: that inherited Rolex and perhaps even the house they always lived in. Eve then would not own the house or half the house (unless he lawfully provided so in his will, but assume he did not). It would be to the southeast—or right-side of the map, as SP—but now would be, more importantly, part of Adam's estate as a whole.

Assume Eve owns half the house because it *was* CP. She doesn't naturally own the other half. It's part of Adam's estate. Now it'd be to the left of the drawing, in those southwestern parishes that used to be his CP interest. But it's still in the bottom half—in the horizontal rectangle—because it's in *his* estate. It just got there from formerly being CP, but either way it's part of the estate, and not part of her property.

The former CP that is now Eve's own property isn't labeled above anymore, because it isn't part of Adam's estate. His death without a will doesn't transfer title to anyone, by operation of law. For our purposes, more importantly, her own property—and it's now hers, at the moment of death—is not affected *even by his will* because it's not his to give. Nor can he give away *her* separate ownership of, say, Arkansas.

Fig. 5 raises all sorts of issues when he has a will, or not. One issue common to those situations is that Eve is not totally SOL. She still has a *usufruct* in the house they shared as community property (we assumed), and in any other former CP. She owns half outright, plus she has a personal-servitude interest in the other half. Practically speaking, that means she can still live in the house until she dies or remarries, whichever comes first (p. 458). Or he may have a will that changes these rules (p. 489), either in her favor (e.g., extending it past remarriage, or granting a usufruct over his SP), or not (even eliminating her default usufruct).

Under the default rules without his changing them by will, this means that she is the owner of half of the former CP—but there are other, "naked," owners of the other half. They have responsibilities to each other, and many rules apply, but the key for now is to understand what's in Adam's own estate. The usufruct that is created by law (or modified by testament) governs her *use* of the property, as detailed in ch. 9, but our focus now is about ownership and what's part of his estate.

There's a common test situation where you need to sort out this math: when you're tested on a small-succession question whether the decedent's estate qualifies. Assuming it's not from out-of-state or so old that exceptions apply (p. 564), the total estate of Louisiana property has to be $125,000 or less at the moment of death. The key is *not* to include her former CP value in that, or any SP she has. So, if Adam's 10k watch is his only SP, and the house that was CP (his only other possession) is worth $200,000—and there's no will—the heirs *can* use succession-by-affidavit instead of court. Why? His estate is worth a gross value of $110,000, which is under the cap.

The issue may also be tested in a direct way without linking it to small-succession eligibility, by asking what Adam's estate is worth in the above example. Answer: $110,000. Read the question carefully, though, since it may make you do the math to include her interest (which isn't the way a court would do it, but they're just making you add the numbers without making it have a legal import). If we include her share, the value of the assets (his estate plus her former CP interest in the one shared asset) is $210,000. These can be tricky, but hopefully sorting out SP from CP and then understanding what's *his* estate at the time of death will make the math simple.

Other than the usufruct, there's other repercussions from the above division of property and its effect on wills and successions. The main one is "forced heirship." We're assuming Adam had children (whether with Eve or otherwise). They were first in line to inherit if there's no will, whatever their age (p. 457). But if there's a will (and *only* if so), rules of forced heirship kick in. The testator can control, *to a point*, how much of the estate goes to whatever recipient they choose. The "to a point" is forced heirship—a rule that forces a minimum percentage of the estate, whatever the will says, to go to the decedent's living children under 24 (up to that minute, in fact, so: 23 + 364.99 days). Or to those otherwise forced by law (mainly disabled children, whatever their age (pp. 484-86), with even some grandchildren included in exceptional cases). There are only eight, limited grounds on which a testator can override the "force" and disinherit an eligible child (pp. 495-96, often tested).

The above "to a point" and "minimum percentage" may sound vague. No, it's just that the minimum amount—the "forced portion" (or "legitime")—*varies* according to how many children the testator has, especially how many of them are forced heirs (under 24 or disabled, and not validly disinherited). Now, assume *one eligible kid:*

17 • VISUALIZING COMMUNITY PROPERTY AND WILLS

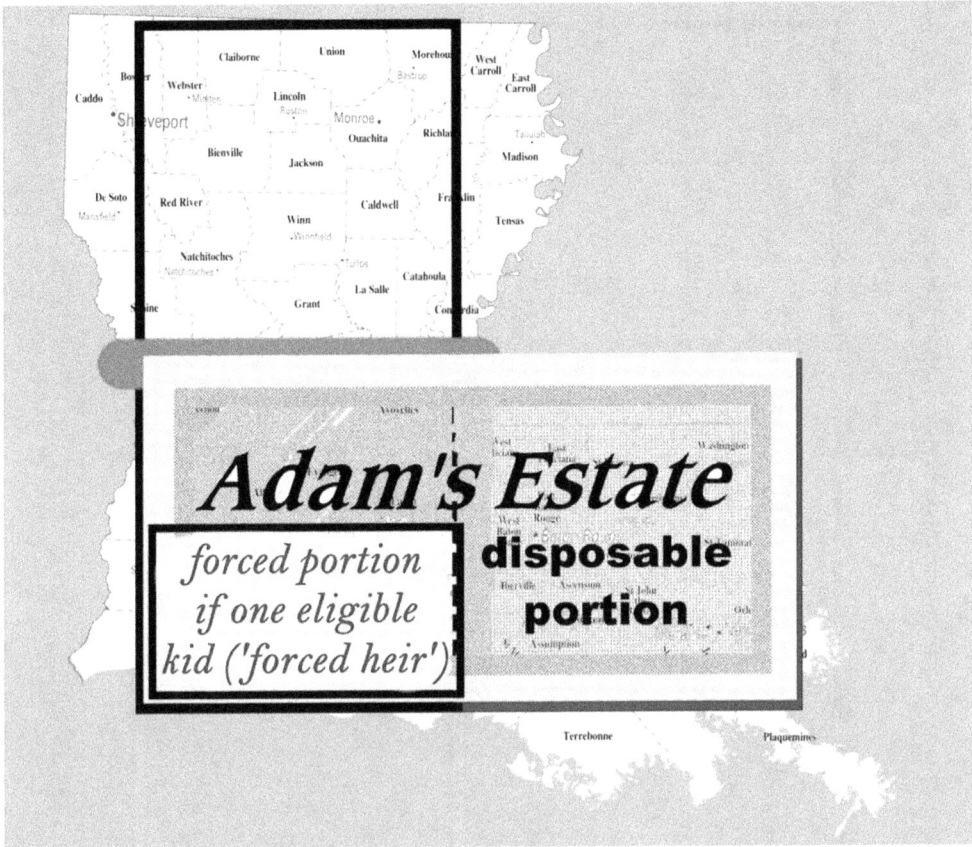

Fig. 6: What *must* be reserved to a forced heir ... if there's *one*

The lone heir (oddly called an "heir" since this only happens with a will, so shouldn't it be *forced legatee*?) must receive, as the "forced portion," one-fourth of Adam's estate. See p. 484.

The rest of his estate (in gray) is the "disposable portion"—because he is free to donate it to Eve, or Octagon Fight Club, other children instead, or whoever/whatever. He could even donate it into a pet trust (p. 525) to the exclusion of the child—up to a point. That point is the forced portion.

Admittedly, now we're getting into the weeds a little. If you understand what is Adam's estate and how CP vs. SP fits into determining that at the time of his death, you're ahead of the game. Most testing should focus on the concept and, perhaps, some math that follows. But be ready for the next-level question: what to do about a forced heir. The simplest such situation involves one forced heir, above.

The percentages change if there's more than one forced heir. Then the forced portion is one-half of the estate. The testator, Adam, is free to dispose of only half his estate (of which a big part may itself be only half of his former CP). That's limited control. Perhaps it's a good reason to have an only child: more control over your estate!

Fig. 7: The forced portion if two or more forced heirs

The example is simple, though perhaps tough on Adam's free will (literally), if there are exactly two forced heirs. They split the half of the estate assigned to the forced portion. With three forced heirs: they split the half three ways. With four forced heirs, still one-half is split, this time four ways; the other half is freely disposable. But there comes a point where the rules of forced heirship would give one child way too much compared to other, non-forced, children. An obscure rule kicks in, then:

The default rules of intestancy would've been unfair to the children *as a whole* if, now that there's a will, one lone forced heir takes over for the non-forced ones (say, the several over age 24). That would be youngest-child-syndrome on steroids! We should limit the forced portion of the amazing-super-lucky child—still protected, but only to a point—to the amount he'd receive if Adam *had* died intestate. I say "he" because I'm thinking of Joseph and his jealous, not-so-lucky brothers (though I realize he wasn't Adam's son nor actually the youngest, and so this analogy is going off the rails). Anyway, Joseph shouldn't take it all (well, the quarter), just because he's the only forced child—leaving the remaining, unforced brothers with not much left to split, if there are several.

17 • VISUALIZING COMMUNITY PROPERTY AND WILLS

To expand on the example in the study guide (p. 484): where the decedent has five kids, and four are not forced heirs (so the forced portion normally follows Fig. 6, for one forced heir: 25%), the *actual* forced portion is 20%: what he'd get in intestacy. The other children could get less by comparison, but not ridiculously so (yes, the four could split the 80% left over, and equal the forced heir, but also could wind up splitting less if Adam leaves something to the Octagon people or to Eve). Of course, because the 80% is the *disposable* portion, and the four older brothers are not forced, Adam can cut them out entirely, by will. That wouldn't happen in intestacy. At any rate, whatever happens to the disposable portion, Joseph doesn't get "too much." Look for this rule to kick in only if the scenario has lots of siblings.

That's the forest of property and testaments, and some trees as well. Most of the details in ch. 24 follow from this structure. What's in the estate is determined from the testator's death, is given immediate ownership to heirs or legatees by seizin, but has to be sorted out as a final matter—to close succession or to allow a succession-by-affidavit—through the rules of intestacy or testacy. If there's a will, there's a place for the notary, both in drafting and in emceeing the signing itself. The will must conform to all the formalities and language of an authentic act (plus, with wording specifically required for such wills, like the attestation clause). But, *stepping back*, the entire concept of donating property after one dies is not just about dotting the i's in a document, it's about dealing with the property as it exists under law. That requires understanding what property is in the estate—and who may receive (and what portion) by default rules of intestacy or, especially, under a valid will.

Fortunately for exam purposes, and even in notary practice, you're not expected to know every nuance, rule, or exception that plays out in court during the succession process. The book in fact warns you not to involve yourself in judicial successions (p. 564), just succession-by-affidavit. You don't need to account for forced heirs when constructing the will—the testator may not know whether they'll have 0 or 12 forced heirs at death, when the determination is made—or for that matter, the value of the estate, then. You just have to have a sense of it to understand the disposable portion the testator ultimately controls. And know the rules of community property because of the ways they can come up on the exam.

A good grip on the right way to construct a will, consistent with the testator's wishes and a correct sorting of the property at stake, will make the grade. Don't be intimidated.

18

Acts, Forms, and Exemplars

The sample acts and forms provided here aren't meant to be comprehensive. These are some of the main ones likely to be useful on exam day, yet the extra pages at the back of *Fundamentals* allow you to handwrite more than just these if you wish. Still, I hope these are a good start. And that by annotating some of them further with marginal notes and the like, they're more useful to understand how these acts work, especially the authentic ones.

The first isn't the most important or testable one, but it's a fair example of a simple affidavit. The study guide doesn't quite provide any other than those related to more core topics such as witness acknowledgments (and a barebones form in ch. 19). Mainly it fits here on a short page, so I've gone ahead and shown one. This could be handwritten at p. 361 or 367. Then, we present one annotated.

<u>AFFIDAVIT OF TRANSLATION</u>

STATE OF LOUISIANA

PARISH OF LINCOLN

BEFORE ME, the undersigned duly commissioned and qualified Notary Public, came and appeared the undersigned

PETER GENE HERNANDEZ

who, after being first duly sworn, did depose and say:

THAT he is fluent in the Tagalog language, that he performs under the professional name Bruno Mars, and that the foregoing is an accurate, true, and complete translation of the document attached hereto, entitled "Minutes of Meeting of Corporate Board of Directors, Bank of West Manila, June 12, 2022."

_____

Peter Gene Hernandez, Affiant

SWORN TO AND SUBSCRIBED BEFORE ME

This <u>9th</u> day of <u>February</u>, 20<u>25</u>

_____

Jamie Lee Curtis, Notary Public
La. Notary ID No. 112233

AFFIDAVIT ← heading

STATE OF LOUISIANA

PARISH OF EAST BATON ROUGE → venue clause (where it's signed)

← officer before whom statement is made

BEFORE ME, the undersigned Notary Public, duly commissioned and qualified in the parish and state aforesaid, came and appeared the undersigned

RICHARD TIFFANY GERE ← appearance of affiant

who, after being first duly sworn, deposed and said: ← "evidence of oath"

1. He is of the age of majority and is domiciled in Rapides Parish, Louisiana. (part of appearance)

2. [Factual assertion here.]

3. [Factual assertion here.] → core content: the declaration or "deposition"

_____ ← signed in presence of officer (notary)
RICHARD TIFFANY GERE, Affiant   (and that's his actual middle name)
← name typed or printed

SWORN TO AND SUBSCRIBED BEFORE ME ← "jurat" is all-important

This _____ day of _____, 20____ ← date of statement (part of jurat)

_____ ← notary signature
Adam Ant, Notary Public ← name typed or printed
Bar Roll No. 12345 ← required (or notary ID #)
Commissioned for Life

typically a stamp goes here

18 • ACTS AND FORMS

WITNESS ACKNOWLEDGMENT ← *heading*

STATE OF LOUISIANA

PARISH OF JEFFERSON

venue: where executed ("SS" here doesn't mean social security)

just means you verified ID if not personally acquainted

BEFORE ME, the undersigned duly commissioned and qualified Notary Public, came and appeared the undersigned person to me known to be the person described in and who executed the foregoing instrument as a witness thereto and acknowledged that she executed the same as her own free act and deed as such witness.

And affiant, being duly sworn did depose and say that such instrument was executed by the parties thereto in the presence of affiant and the other subscribing witnesses and by all parties thereto of their own free act and deed for the uses, considerations, and purposes therein expressed.

_____
LOUISA MAY ALCOTT, Affiant

jurat

SWORN TO AND SUBSCRIBED BEFORE ME

This _____ day of _____, 20____, at Metairie, Louisiana.

- *form used to complete an "authenticated act" that was executed by parties who now can't BOTH appear before notary, so: original witness to signing comes in and "acknowledges" the original instrument...*
- *not quite an "authentic act" but has evidentiary qualities of one (it's "self-proving")*

_____
TONYA MAXINE HARDING, Notary Public
Louisiana Notary ID No. 66666

119

DONATION INTER VIVOS OF IMMOVABLE

(as opposed to "donation mortis causa," i.e., a will)

STATE OF LOUISIANA

PARISH OF ST. CHARLES

venue clause: it's where document is executed, not location of property (or where filed)

BEFORE ME, the undersigned notary, duly commissioned and qualified in the parish and aforesaid, and in the presence of the two witnesses whose names are hereunto subscribed, PERSONALLY CAME and appeared: — *preamble*

[Donor(s) appearance clause(s) reciting (a) full name, domicile, and permanent mailing address of the donor(s); (b) marital status of all donors who are individuals, including full name of the present spouse or a declaration that the party is unmarried; and (c) a declaration as to whether there has been a change in the marital status of any party who is a donor of the immovable or interest or right since (s)he acquired it, and if so, when and in what manner the change occurred.] — *appearance clause of donor*

Herein DONOR, whether singular or plural who declared that [CAUSE, DEPENDING ON FACTS (e.g., ". . .in consideration of the natural love and affection that he has for DONEE, his nephew," or ". . . in consideration of his support for the improvement of educational opportunities for students of Tulane Law School"),] — *such "cause" need not impose conditions*

said DONOR did and by these presents does, give, grant, convey, donate, assign, set over and deliver unto — *clear intent to give, effective now*

[Donee(s) appearance clause(s) reciting (a) the full name, domicile, and permanent mailing address of the donee(s); (b) the marital status of all donees who are individuals, including full name of the present spouse or a declaration that the party is unmarried.]

Herein DONEE, whether singular or plural, here present and accepting with gratitude, for himself, his successors and assigns, and acknowledging due delivery and possession thereof, as a donation, the following described property: — *donee does not have to appear now, but must accept in writing to make effective (usually)*

[Legal property description, including the municipal number or postal address of the property if it has one.] **description, not just address**

The parties hereto estimate the value of said donated property in the amount of _____ dollars ($_____.__ USD), and DONOR declares that the property hereby donated by him does not exceed the disposable portion of his estate.

To have and to hold the said property unto the donee(s), his heirs, successors and assigns, in full ownership forever, with full and general warranty of title, and with full substitution and subrogation to all rights and actions of warranty which said donor may have against all former owners or vendors of said property.

All taxes due on said property have been paid, as evidenced by tax certificate attached hereto. Further tax notices shall be sent to donee at [address].

The parties hereto waive and dispense with the production of any mortgage, conveyance, or other certificates, required by law, and relieve and release me, notary, from any and all connection therewith.

18 ▪ ACTS AND FORMS

This act is passed before me, notary, without a request for examination of title and none was made. The description herein was furnished to me, notary, by the parties, and the parties relieve and release me from any and all liability in connection therewith, forever holding me, notary, and my heirs and successors harmless from any and all claims forever.

Said donor stipulates that the aforesaid property has not heretofore been alienated by him and is free of all encumbrances.

THUS DONE, READ AND PASSED at my office in the City of Hahnville, Louisiana, on the _____ day of _____, 20____ in the presence of the two undersigned competent witnesses who hereunto sign their names together with said appearers and me, notary.

WITNESSES:

_____   _____, DONOR

[Type/print W1 name under signature]   [Type/print DONOR name under signature]

_____   _____, DONEE

[Type/print W2 name under signature]   [Type/print DONEE name under signature]

_____

[Type/print name under signature], Notary Public

Notary ID No. _____

Note: Although the above authentic act assumes that Donee is present and signs, which is typical, the donation may also be completed and effective by the Donee's acceptance later, in writing (usually). Acceptance need not be an authentic act nor necessarily a part of THIS authentic act. If Donee is not present, the above Appearance Clause would be adjusted so as not to say s(he)'s here. In the written acceptance, Donee needs to be clear they are accepting this donation, much like the above. The Study Guide lists some atypical situations where acceptance is completed by action rather than in writing.

LOUISIANA NOTARY EXAM SIDEPIECE TO THE 2025 STUDY GUIDE

STATE OF LOUISIANA } *venue clause*
PARISH OF JEFFERSON }

LAST WILL AND TESTAMENT

OF

[TESTATOR FULL NAME]

↳ *what constitutes a "full name" & when required? See R.S. 35:12*

BE IT KNOWN, that before me, the undersigned authority, duly commissioned and qualified in and for the Parish of Jefferson, State of Louisiana, and in the presence of the undersigned competent witnesses, personally came and appeared: *preamble: not necessarily required as long as testator's appearance clause appears in his or her statement (after "I")*

[TESTATOR FULL NAME], of the full age of majority, who declared that (s)he lives and resides in the Parish of Jefferson, Louisiana at the following address: [street address, city, LA, zip] *appearance of testator uses residence address instead of domicile, unlike most authentic acts*

who declared to me, Notary, that (s)he wishes to take advantage of the provisions of La. Civ. Code Ann. art. 1576, et seq., and does hereby make and declare this to be his/her last will and testament:

La. courts prefer this to "being of sound mind"

I, [FULL NAME], being able to comprehend generally the nature and consequences of this act, realizing the precarious and uncertain nature of life, and wishing to dispose of all the property which I may own at the time of my death by Last Will and Testament, knowing how and being able to read and write, declare this to be my final testament. I revoke all of my prior testaments or codicils.   ↳ *capacity*

I.

Marriage. I, [FULL NAME], have been married twice, first to [NAME], from whom I am divorced, and second to [NAME], from whom I am divorced. I have no minor children or forced heirs. *marital history and current status are also part of T's appearance*

DISPOSITIVE PORTION starts here

II.

A) Specific Bequest. As a specific bequest, I give, will, and bequest the *full and complete ownership* of my box of files to [NAME 1], my granddaughter, so that she may finalize my estate.

B) As an additional specific bequest, I give the *full and complete ownership* of the bank accounts and any stocks in my name to [NAME 2].   ↳ *a particular legacy*

C) I give, will and bequeath the *full and complete ownership* all of the rest of my property to [NAME 3]. If she should predecease me, then the property should go to [NAME 1].   ↳ *universal legacy*

valuable opportunity to appoint one and define duties

III.

A) Executor. I appoint [NAME 1] as Executrix of my succession to serve with full seizin and without bond. Should she cease or fail to serve, I name [NAME 3] as successor Executrix. All of my executors may serve as independent administrators, without court supervision. In accordance with Louisiana Civil Code Article 1572, my executors are authorized to allocate specific assets to satisfy a legacy. All of my executors have my express authority to serve as "independent executors."

signature of T
_____

signature, not just initials, at end of each page [testator name]   page 1 of 2

B) Compensation. My individual Executrix shall serve without compensation, but shall be entitled to recover his or her expenses from my Estate.

C) Bond. I dispense all of my Executors, including any duly appointed dative or provisional executor, from giving bond.

D) Selection of Assets. Pursuant to La. Civ. Code art. 1572, my executor has the authority to select assets to satisfy any legacy herein expressed as a quantum or value of my estate, including a fractional share.

E) Common disaster. Should I die together with any legatee in a common disaster or under such circumstances as to render it doubtful as to who died first, it shall be presumed that I survived. *protect against who-died-first*

F) Collation. I dispense all of my heirs from collating any gift received from me whether inter vivos or by reason of my death.

G) Undue Influence. No disposition in this testament has been made by me as a result of hatred, anger, suggestion or captation. I understand the nature and extent of my property and the consequences of the dispositions in this testament.

H) Should any of the provisions of this will be for any reason declared invalid, such invalidity shall not affect any of the other provisions of this will and all invalid provisions shall be wholly disregarded in interpreting this will.

Date: _____   *Signature of T*
                                          [Testator name below signature] *type/print full name*

ATTESTATION CLAUSE: Use exact language of C.C. art. 1577, if possible:
In our presence the testator has declared or signified that this instrument is his/her testament and has signed it at the end and on each other separate page, and in the presence of the testator and each other we have hereunto subscribed our names this ____ day of *[date is crucial]* 20____ at [city], LA.

WITNESSES:

Signature of W1   *Signature of W2*
[Witness #1 name printed/typed here]   [Witness #2 name printed/typed here]

                    Notary's Signature
            [Notary's name printed or typed below signature] ⎤ *statutory*
                    Bar Roll No. 12345*   ⎬ *requirements,*
                    My Commission is for Life   ⎦ *see R.S. 35:12(B)*

| STAMP |
| TYPICALLY |
| HERE |

* Use Notary ID number if not an attorney-notary

POWER OF ATTORNEY

BY ERIC T. JONES

IN FAVOR OF GREG R. MENDEL

UNITED STATES OF AMERICA

STATE OF LOUISIANA

PARISH OF ST. TAMMANY

BE IT KNOWN that on _____, 20____, before me, _____, a notary public duly qualified in and for the above stated state and parish, and in the presence of the named and undersigned competent witnesses, personally appeared ERIC T. JONES, a person over the age of majority and a resident and domiciliary of St. Tammany Parish, Louisiana, "principal," who declared under oath that he has been married once to Nancy Drew, from whom he is widowed, and has not since remarried, and whose mailing address is 123 Baker St., Abita Springs, LA 70420, and who declared that he appoints GREG R. MENDEL as attorney-in-fact or agent, to perform the acts authorized in this power of attorney, hereinafter referred to as "agent," to be his agent, mandatary, and attorney-in-fact, with full power and authority to act for, in the name of and on behalf of principal, to do all acts necessary or deemed by agent to be appropriate to represent principal including, but not limited to, the following:

1. Business and Affairs. To conduct, manage, and transact the business and personal financial matters of principal, of every nature and kind without any exception.

2. Correspondence. To open all letters, emails, facsimiles, and other correspondence, electronic or otherwise, addressed to principal and to answer same in principal's name.

3. Banking. To make and endorse and to accept and to pay promissory notes, drafts, and bills of exchange; to sign checks …. [more on banking actions allowed]

4. Securities. To sell, purchase, and transfer shares of stock, bonds, or any other securities of any corporation or any other legal entity ….

5. Loans. To borrow money in principal's name from any bank or other financial institution; to make, issue, and endorse any promissory note ….

6. Property: Sale, Purchase, Lease, Mortgage, Pledge. To sell, mortgage, encumber, pledge, purchase, lease, or grant servitudes pertaining to immovable (real) or movable (personal) property, although not described in this instrument as permitted by Louisiana Civil Code Annot. art. 2996 on such terms and conditions as determined by agent and to execute such documents to effect such acts and receive or pay amounts pursuant to such acts; this authority and discretion expressly includes the property located at 123 Baker St., Abita Springs, LA 70420, and any automobiles.

7. Judicial Proceedings. To appear before all courts ….

8. Successions. To represent principal judicially and otherwise ….

Page 1 of 3

9. Claims. To demand and obtain and to recover and take receipt for ....

10. Donations. To transfer without consideration (i.e., donate) any asset of principal to any person as determined by agent.

11. Tax Returns and Related Matters. To file any United States, Louisiana or other tax returns (including, but not limited to, income tax returns); to apply for extensions ....

12. General. To do and perform each and every other act, matter or thing as may be appropriate in agent's discretion as if such act, matter or thing were or had been particularly stated in this instrument.

13. Substitute Agent. Principal grants the co-agents by joint agreement the power to appoint and remove a substitute agent, which appointment will be by authentic act.

14. Liability of Agent. Agent will be liable only for breach of duty to principal committed in bad faith. Principal will indemnify agent and hold agent harmless for all reasonable costs, fees and expenses regarding all matters in this contract, legal actions brought by or against the agent for which agent is not liable within the standard specified in this section. No further compensation shall be allowed.

15. Reliance. This power of attorney and any substitute power of attorney executed pursuant to Section 17, above, may be filed and recorded with the clerk of court for St. Tammany Parish and registered in the conveyance records, and will remain in effect as to third persons dealing with the agent until either the power or substitute power of attorney is revoked by notarial act and recorded as set forth above, and/or the third person receives actual notice of revocation. If any party who relies on this power of attorney delivers written notice to the principal, this power of attorney will remain in effect until the party receives written notice of revocation, notwithstanding recordation of revocation as stated above.

THUS DONE AND PASSED, on the day, month, and year first above written, in the presence of the undersigned competent witnesses who have signed their names together with the principal and me, notary.

I understand the full import of this designation, and I am emotionally and mentally competent to make this appointment and grant these powers and authorities.

_____

ERIC T. JONES, Principal

Witnesses:

_____	_____
Witness signature	Witness signature
_____	_____
Printed name of W1	Printed name of W2

_____
Notary Printed Name _____
Notary ID Number _____

    The undersigned accepts the appointment created by this power of attorney to act as the principal's true and lawful agent, mandatary, and attorney-in-fact.

_____

GREG R. MENDEL, Agent

Note: Agent does not have to appear with Principal or be witnessed accepting, especially since the appearance clause only says Principal appears; witnesses are used here because POA grants the power of donation.

BILL OF SALE OF A MOVABLE

STATE OF LOUISIANA
PARISH OF _____

    BEFORE ME, the undersigned Notary Public, duly commissioned and qualified in and for the parish and state aforesaid, personally came and appeared:

_____ ,

Seller, of legal age, who hereby sells and delivers with full and general warranty of title unto:

_____ ,

Buyer, of legal age, the following movable property:

    Make:

    Model: Color:

    Year:

    VIN:

    Vehicle Sale Price: Date of Sale:

Seller warrants that there are no mortgages, liens or encumbrances of any kind against the movable property sold or any accessories attached thereon.

Signed on this _____ day of _____ , year of 20____ .

                                      signed here _____
                                      Seller
                                      signed here _____
                                      Buyer

                                      _____
                                      _____ (print name),
                                      Notary Public, ID # _____

19

Notarial Practice Tips

Once you've passed and received your commission, here are some practice tips or answers to day-to-day questions that the study guide does not fully share. For that reason, not all of the advisories below will be on the exam (though they bring a practicality to some transactions and forms that they may help you remember items that *are* in the study guide and get tested). At least, you may want to have these suggestions around when you do start your career as a practicing notary, or are already qualified as one due to bar membership. My wife Michele and I have learned them mainly through our notary practice, asking around, Facebook groups, or books we've read (some listed in one of the items below).[*]

Your signature is your seal. But. The study guide does make clear that no more than your signature is required to complete the notarization process (p. 74). That fact has been tested, probably because it's counterintuitive that a state so steeped in formalities and ritual is fine with a less-formal 'seal' than most states use. The study guide suggests that end-users, especially out-of-state recipients of notarized documents, don't *know* that a signature is enough (also p. 74). Or *their* state law won't allow a mere signature. So they may reject the forms. For this reason, notaries have official stamps and embossers made and keep them handy (such as a second set in the car). Moreover, clients *expect* them, even Louisiana ones.

Where to get stamps. Quality and affordable stamps and embossers can be found from many local rubberstamp companies (like Ed Smith Stencil Works in New Orleans), online notary stores, and even Amazon. In our experience, Trodat brand embossers fit better in your hand than most other inexpensive brands. A paired stamp and embosser run about $49 online. Mail-order embossers tend to be a bit tricky to assemble, in that you may think the device is properly seated when it really isn't.

Other stamps. In addition to the basic stamp that has your name, parish, state, and notary ID number, practitioners find it useful to get a few made that they use a lot more than they'd guess. One is "A True Copy" stamp, to certify copies of documents you yourself originated (pp. 611-12). Another is a jurat stamp ("Sworn to and subscribed..."; see p. 616) that pretty much turns a client's letter or statement they've prepared into a mini-affidavit—at least sufficient to satisfy a

---

[*] In 2021, we began teaching a webinar called "I Passed—Now What?" to answer these and many other questions about starting practice as a notary; see *www.schoolofnotary.com*. Organizations such as the Louisiana Notary Association, noted below in this chapter, also present occasional shop talks on tips for new notaries.

school, landlord, sporting league, or other entity that wants a notarized statement of fact (such as a statement of residence address) and is not looking for a formal courtroom-style affidavit. Michele and I use a jurat stamp a lot.

Certified birth certificates or official records. You can't make a "true copy" of birth certificates, death certificates, and the like—"certifying" those is up to the bureau of vital statistics (p. 613). So: what to do when a school or recreational organization requires "a notarized birth certificate"? Or someone similarly is asking for an official record to be formalized? The ready solution, which satisfies most such requests, is for *the client* to state that it is an exact copy and sign that statement, and for you to use the jurat stamp (or a jurat you write onto the copy) to show that they have sworn to the fact before you. Adding your signature and your notary stamp should suffice. So, the safe route is to state it in the form of the client's own brief affidavit. By the way, you can't legally photocopy at all some naturalization documents (they say so on the paper), much less certify them as a true copy.

What do "seal" and "SS" mean on a form? Many forms that require notarization have a special place marked "seal." Sometimes that means "signature," like when it's just a line. Yet, they're probably looking for an actual stamp or embossing, not just your signature (despite Louisiana law, above). To be cautious, most practitioners use both stamp and embossing near that spot, and physically sign the form too on the appropriate line. As for "SS," usually found near the venue clause, that's *not* asking for a social security number; it's short for a Latin phrase that means "namely" or "to wit," and can just be ignored.

What if a form asks for the end-date of my commission? Forms often do that, because every other state uses limited terms. Don't leave the line blank (after "Commission expires ___"), or they may think yours expired. Fill in "lifetime," or "on death." (Michele sometimes writes "when I do.") Some stamps or stock forms say it, too: "My Commission is for Life," below the notary's name/ID number. On forms, you may even have to write LIFETIME over a line like "___/___/___."

Where do I emboss if there's no space for it? NOT over the signatures, dates, or other features that are meant to be part of the notarization ritual. Use the margin if you need to, and at worst emboss over some unimportant words in the document. If there's room, ideally the stamp and/or embossing go *below* your signature, after signing. Because so many forms leave little space for the stamp (such as vehicle titles), I bought one online that's smaller than the more formal ones I use more.

What if a document is meant to be faxed or scanned after notarization? The embossing alone won't show well after scanning and the recipient may think it was not stamped. Using both a stamp and an embosser solves the issue. Some use a different, round stamp that looks like inked embossing (and don't further emboss it). Others use a gold, round label stuck to the paper and then emboss over it. In reality, the basic (rectangular) rubberstamp is fine.

19 ▪ NOTARIAL PRACTICE TIPS

What if you make an error on a document a client brings you? This will happen. It's best to make a copy before working on anything halfway complicated, or at least ask if the customer has the original in an email they could access (so it can be recreated if the first one is marred, for instance by writing the names in the wrong place). White-out is never allowed. If the document is a certificate of title, there's a detailed (and tested) process using an affidavit of correction (p. 439) that must be done for all errors, even small ones, or just to strike out something goofy on the back. For less official and immutable documents, usually a cross-through correction by the notary, initialed by the notary, will fix it.

What if the form says "County of" instead of "Parish of"? You certainly *could* cross out the word and replace it with the proper Louisiana unit. Many notaries routinely do and they're right to say the document remains valid. But we've found that some out-of-state recipients of documents they don't want to honor quickly (such as a lien release that means the recipient now has to pay a contractor) may look for any excuse to say the form was altered and is no longer valid. We suggest not crossing it out, but simply filling the blank with, say, Caddo Parish. It's odd to say "County of Caddo Parish ," sure, but the form will at least be honored. This is like the fact that "your signature is your seal": you know that's law, but if the recipient doesn't believe you, what good is being right? Similarly, don't insist on teaching a recipient a geography lesson when the only goal should be to have the notarization recognized.

What if the client has signed the form before they see you? They often think they are doing you a favor, or saving time, to go ahead and sign it before you see them. If they have another original they can sign in front of you, that's ideal, but it's usually satisfactory to have them sign the form again in your presence (even at the bottom of the page). The book provides case law (p. 334) that suggests a signer of an affidavit can *confirm* their signature to you if they already signed it. But really there's no reason to create an issue when it's possible to have them sign the document in your presence even if they signed it previously.

What if the client signs as an agent or mandatary on behalf of a principal? Be sure to instruct them to sign the document with their *own* name, and not "forge" the principal's name on the signature line. It's intuitive to clients that the form is asking for the principal's name to be signed, even if they have to do it "for" the principal. But that's wrong, and they probably need to be specifically told to sign their own name before they put pen to paper—and invalidate the form, which may be the one copy they have. Make sure they have a POA (or are listed on the SOS website as qualified for a company), to show their capacity to sign.

What to do if they don't have one of the listed IDs? P. 74 lists the four forms of ID which suffice (unless you know the client well, or someone you know well vouches for their identity, in which case they can forego ID). If they don't have that ID, don't assume they are who they say they are. The easiest ways to commit professional malpractice are to allow a signer to talk you into ignoring their lack of ID or to fail to have the person physically in front of you when they sign. But those four listed IDs aren't the only acceptable documents to verify identity (e.g., a non-U.S. passport with photo, checked on Google as proper for that nation). The key is for you to use a process and proof that reasonably establish identity. Also, 'LA Wallet' says it's discretionary to the notary whether to accept it.

Where to check out-of-state IDs to be sure they're real? There are huge, expensive books sold that cover all sorts of identifications with pictures and updates. For nearly all notary purposes, though, Google is your friend and does the trick.

Forms that say "personally known to me" when I don't know the person? For most forms, that just means that they became personally known to you because you checked the appropriate ID above (or actually do know them). They don't expect you to attest to signatures only of people you knew before they came through the door. Other forms, more helpfully, list in the alternative "personally known to me *or* identified by ____" where you are expected to fill in the blank with "LA driver's license" or similar (or underline "personally known" if they really are, then cross a line above their blank line, so you don't make it seem like neither applies). We make a practice of filling in not only the form of ID but the number on it ("LA driver lic 2751662") so that the user *knows* we checked.

Blanks in forms? You're not supposed to let the form be signed before its blanks are filled in (pp. 650-51). That seems most crucial in cases where the missing information is something they are attesting to, and not just informational like their phone number. In any event, the end product needs to have blanks filled in, with lines to show the blank was considered but ignored, or use of "N/A" and "none" to explain the omitted data. Certainly you can't notarize essentially a blank form or document, especially with affidavits, authentic acts, and other instruments where the signing is the last part of the ritual that makes it legally valid.

Using ordinals when filling in dates? It's not necessary to write the th in "6th day of March, 2025" when filling blanks by hand in acts or forms. The 6 alone will do. Exception for number 1: we do write 1st instead of 1, just because the lone mark may look like it's not fully marked in, so adding some characters there makes it clear it's the 'first.' Also it's less easily changed by the client later.

Take your time. Don't be afraid to ask a client to come back after you've researched and drafted the matter rather than trying to impress them by doing it on the spot. Even with a form the client brings in, use the official study guide and its sequels to look up a subject area rather than going by memory. Of course you'd recall when confronted by two parents and a baby that the state form for acknowledging paternity is an authentic act. But without looking at the guide's section on this monumental moment (p. 599), you may not recall that you have to read, and give in writing, specific warnings to the parents, if not the baby.

Organizations to join. Both the Louisiana Notary Association (LNA.org) and the Professional Civil Law Notaries Association (PCLNA.org) are excellent professional groups which offer continuing education, newsletters, legislative updates, forms, and networking. It appears that the live seminars or meetings that they routinely offer are geared more for southern Louisiana with LNA and northern Louisiana with PCLNA, but really both groups have members statewide.

Where to get more forms and exemplars? Sets of forms, acts, and examples for many situations can be purchased from many sources, including downloadable sources, and in notebook form from the Louisiana Notary Association (their latest *Notary Survival Kit*). All sorts of forms, bills of sale, and sample acts can be found online with a search—but that doesn't mean they're valid or well done. And resources of various prep courses (such as the PassMyNotary workbooks) include some forms. In all cases, be sure you are using a form that is for Louisiana. Other states are too different.

For a more comprehensive collection of Louisiana-specific forms, Michele and I published a book at Amazon or B&N of more than 170 forms for a large variety of situations. It is *Louisiana Notary and Legal Forms with Explanations*, and we add introductions and footnotes to explain how to adapt them to a client's need. (It is also available separately as downloadable, formatted Word files from our website.) West Publishing produces a comprehensive book, *Louisiana Notary Handbook*, but since it costs over $950, the best place to use it may be a parish law library.

Other books to have handy. In addition to the *Survival Kit* or resources like ours that provide many forms, and of course the *Fundamentals* guide and this book, consider having a recent edition of the Louisiana Civil Code on your shelf. The LNA offers one by a leading law publisher—West—at a discount price for members. We also recommend a brief, clear, and inexpensive book (at Amazon and the like): Rome & Kinsella, *Louisiana Civil Law Dictionary* (2011). The National Notary Association's *Notary Home Study Course* is actually a useful book to read as you embark in the profession—and surprisingly: (1) much of its advice is useful even in Louisiana, especially the attesting-to-signatures part, and (2) despite its title, it's not so much about studying for a future exam as it is about the day-to-day work of a notary on a very practical level.

For exam prep, I'd be remiss if I didn't recommend to you (beside ours class) my extensive but affordable quiz workbook, which offers many detailed tips and decodes the 'trick' or logic of how questions are worded. It's titled *Louisiana Notary Exam Sample Questions and Answers 2025*. Its explanations of answers tie page references to the current state study guide.

Should I notarize a will that a customer brings to me that seems to be prepared from an online resource or providers like LegalZoom? Probably not, unless it's clear that it really meets all the requirements of Louisiana testamentary law and accomplishes what the testator intends. You're not doing them any favors by notarizing a will that isn't going to be valid but may add an extra layer of litigation or doubt over having no will at all. Sure signs that they don't get that we're different is when they use the common law phrase "being of sound mind"—or, far worse, they have the testator initial the bottom of pages instead of signing, as Louisiana law absolutely requires. Just say no. However, we don't mind executing a testament well-drafted by a Louisiana attorney.

Wrong signer? It's fairly common for clients to think they're the one to sign the form when it's supposed to be their spouse (as with the consent by non-participant spouse to allow a withdrawal from a retirement plan) or parent (as with a mom's guaranteeing payments to a college dorm). Or they think that one of them can sign it at home and the other bring it to the notary. We've found that the children in the dorm-guarantee situation are often quite insistent that the form was signed by their parent and don't seem to understand that the point of a notary is to *watch* it get signed. There's nothing you can do in such situations but insist, politely, that the correct signer come by.

Negotiation of pricing. Many customers think there's no reason a notary should charge money, especially if they're from other states where notary services are often provided free at banks. The civil law notary is much more than the notary in any other state and deserves to be paid for our professional services. Create a standard, printed-out list of prices for particular services, and stand by it. When clients try to self-discount their particular need from your standard prices (many try), it's tempting to give in, but it's not right—and it tends to become permanent even if you made clear it's a one-time favor. Do it only if there's some larger need of yours that you're serving (such as offering it free as part of a larger transaction for which you're charging), not just as a favor or the path of least resistance. Have a way to accept credit card payments or provide change and receipts.

Don't get suspended. It's embarrassing, though easily fixed, to be suspended because you haven't filed an annual report or otherwise remained technically eligible (such as being actively registered to vote, or renewing your bond). A casual review of actual notary listings on the Secretary of State's website reveals that very many of the non-attorney notaries have been suspended for a brief period at one or two points of their careers. You need to calendar the earliest time that your annual report may be filed and have your phone alert you as well. Don't ignore emails and letters from the Secretariat.

Get E&O coverage and not just a bond. Professional failures and mistakes can occur even if you never mean to. It doesn't cost much more beyond the surety bond (which protects only the Governor) to get Errors & Omissions protection for yourself. Typically a bond bought online or with an agent—it's easy, from many companies—costs about $110 for five years, while an E&O policy (that satisfies the bond requirement, too) is $140 to 150, so we're talking $8 or less difference per year. It may actually save money, as discussed previously at the end of ch. 4. The site *www.notarystamp.com* sells E&Os and bonds, and even applies their discount code (often 10 to 20% off) to them. So you could wind up getting E&O for basically the price of a bond.

How much coverage should I get? The minimum required is $10,000, whether bond or E&O policy. We strongly suggest at least $25,000 in E&O coverage, not only as better protection costing not much more per year, but also because many loan signing services that would otherwise hire you for closings and refinances require that you have that coverage.

19 • NOTARIAL PRACTICE TIPS

Must I be certified to be a loan signing agent? To offer your services as a loan signing agent, the hard part in this state is getting your notary commission. Many companies will retain you for closings and refi's with nothing more, so you probably don't *have* to do more. (We've done many, all without further certification; and it helps that most such closings come with a checklist and specific instructions for the notary.) But some may ask whether you've passed the national "notary signing agent" exam. It's a lot quicker and easier than our notary exam itself, and can be affordably learned through courses such as that offered by the National Notary Association. Whether or not it is *required* to get hired, learning best practices specific to this task is wise, especially if you plan to make loan closings a consistent part of your practice.

The most important tip is in the study guide. On p. 619 and elsewhere the guide suggests that the easiest way to lose your commission and your reputation is to deviate from rules you know to be the case—as by doing someone "a favor," such as notarizing forms dropped off to you already signed by someone not before you. We've had people ask us to confirm over the phone that they gave permission to have someone bring the form by. Maybe they can be forgiven for not understanding what a notary is for. You won't be. Every time you're asked to cut a corner for an employer or customer, remind yourself how challenging this journey is. If you have to, say to *them*: "You have no idea what someone has to go through to become a notary in Louisiana. The exam has a 20% pass rate and costs real money. I'm sorry, I can't risk that for you." If they don't understand *that*, it's a big red flag that maybe they're trying to get you to cut corners for suspicious reasons and not just because they forgot their ID at home.

Some other very important tips are not. Be professional, be patient, never put yourself into a physically (not just legally) vulnerable position, take pride, and have fun.

About the Author

STEVEN ALAN CHILDRESS is a senior professor at Tulane Law School, holding the Conrad Meyer III Professorship in Civil Procedure. He has taught Torts, Evidence, and Legal Profession at Tulane since 1988, in addition to visiting positions with Loyola–New Orleans and George Washington. He also co-teaches the Louisiana Notary Law class in Tulane's School of Professional Advancement. He has lectured for Continuing Legal Education on notary practice, legal ethics, and evidence law, as well as teaching Louisiana Bar Review for a decade.

He earned his law degree from Harvard and a PhD in Jurisprudence from Berkeley. He clerked in Shreveport for the federal court of appeals, then practiced law in California with two national firms. He is a member of the Louisiana Notary Association, the Law & Society Association, and the California and D.C. bar associations. He authored the three-volume treatise *Federal Standards of Review*, (5th ed. 2024), edited three books on legal ethics, and annotated a 2010 edition of Oliver Wendell Holmes's *The Common Law*. More recently, he wrote *Louisiana Notary Exam Sample Questions and Answers*, as well as the introductory guide, *Become a Notary Public in Louisiana*.

Alan is a commissioned Louisiana notary who, along with his wife Michele (an attorney/notary since 2002), owned a notary and shipping service in Jefferson Parish. They have performed thousands of notarial acts covering a wide range of subjects and formats. Alan is also a practicing notary for the Tulane University community. He and Michele offer remote prep seminars, live on Zoom and recorded, through the website *SchoolOfNotary.com*, and co-authored *Louisiana Notary and Legal Forms with Explanations* (2024).

If you have suggestions for test-taking advice, corrections to this guidebook, reflections about current exam topics, or examples where you think the author's strategies can be improved, please email them to *achildress@tulane.edu*.

Visit us at *www.quidprobooks.com*.

www.ingramcontent.com/pod-product-compliance
Lightning Source LLC
Chambersburg PA
CBHW060254240426
43673CB00047B/1928